# Mirror, Mirror . . . Please Lie

by

Pat Wellman

Beacon Hill Press of Kansas City
Kansas City, Missouri

Permission to quote from the following copyrighted versions of the Bible
is acknowledged with appreciation:

From *The Holy Bible, New International Version* (NIV), copyright © 1978 by
    the New York International Bible Society. Used by permission.

From *The Living Bible* (TLB), copyright © 1971 by Tyndale House Publishers,
    Wheaton, Ill. Used by permission.

Unless otherwise indicated all Scripture references are from the NIV.

10 9 8 7 6 5 4 3 2 1

Mirror, Mirror . . .
Please Lie

To Don,
whose life has mirrored the image of God to me
since the day we met

# Contents

# Contents

# Introduction

Is there a woman on earth who can pass a mirror without just one little peek? I doubt it. After all, mirrors tell a lot of things: they affirm, they laugh and cry, they reveal a crooked hemline, they warn us to slow down for the policeman behind us, they make us self-conscious about the messy job the hairdresser did, they make that closet-sized dining room look like a banquet hall, and they give us a pat on the back when we have nicely gotten it all together. But they never lie! Well, almost never. A mirror in one of our bedrooms tells little white ones. It trims me down at least 15 pounds! Do you blame me for getting dressed in its reflection as often as I can? I certainly avoid the one in the other bedroom that unashamedly tells it like it is!

Mirrors are magnetic. I once stood in the middle of a living room carrying on a 20-minute conversation with a woman who talked the whole time to the large mirror behind me. Actually, *she* carried on. I just nodded, hoping my face might become more important to her than the one she saw in the mirror. It never did. We never made eye contact. I sometimes wish I had turned around and talked to the person in the mirror. At least she might have remembered my name.

Men are not altogether innocent. Just for fun (or for rebuttal) station yourself near a mirror in the foyer of a large business building. Who looks most, the men or the women? Fifty, fifty. You can bet on it! No, you can't bet, but you can smile about it!

Abraham Lincoln watched a naval officer at length one time, amused with the constant posing and primping the young man went through in front of the mirror. "You must be a very happy man," stated the president. "You are in love with yourself, and you haven't a rival in the world."

I'm sure God smiles a little at our posing and primping, all the time urging and prodding us toward the discovery of His love that makes it OK, yea, necessary to love ourselves. If only He had scribbled out a definitive picture of me and sent it along with my birth certificate. I know He says He made me in His image. I do believe that, but I wonder then if He, too, has tastebuds for all the wrong things?

Solomon may not have known about mirrors, but he knew about reflection. Maybe he stood at the edge of a body of water as he said, "As water reflects a face, so a man's heart reflects the man." Wise man, that Solomon! He knew that water (and mirrors) offer surface reflections. One must look beyond them both for depth. Beneath the beautiful water of the Pacific, for instance, lurk all kinds of yucky substances.

Now yucky is not a word as easily applied to people, but the application is well taken. Mirrors stubbornly reflect only the substance exposed to them: the outward, visible suitcase that may or may not speak truthfully of its contents.

Some of the most beautiful women in the world are not very pretty when you get to know them. Of *course* I know they are not alone in that predicament; it's just that we expect beauty to be total. Beauty is really magnificent when a beautiful person has found a beautiful body to live in! And you, with me, know some beautiful, beautiful people who have captured our spiritual admiration so much we are hard-pressed to describe them physically.

Solomon knew the greater truth: there is a mirror of the soul, the heart. And he understood its colossal importance for he said, "Above all else, guard your heart, for it is the wellspring of life" (Prov. 4:23).

Everywhere I go and in everything I do I encounter mirrors reflecting my heart condition. When I look and see yucky, I must get down to business with the heart. When I can see beautiful, I rejoice and cherish the fact that God has been at work, and I give thanks! My inner self celebrates the addition of another bit of shading in the total picture.

That's what this book is all about. It is not a how-to book. It comes from my heart with a sincere motive of "let's look and consider together!" It is the putting into print a sampling of hundreds of moments spent "looking" and "reflecting" with various and sundry versions of His image!

For me, the best heart-conditioning formula for producing lovely reflections is found in *The Living Bible* paraphrase of Gal. 6:4. It reads: "Let everyone be sure that he is doing his very best, for then he will have the personal satisfaction of work well done, and won't need to compare himself with someone else."

What I really wish to say concerning this passage makes up the second part of this book. Between here and there, however, is probably the longest introduction you have ever read!

I love you. Thank you for taking a look with me!

# 1

# The Rearview Vision Mirror

SINCE MY HUSBAND was out of town and my son was away at college, those sitting at the supper table were my mother who was visiting, my daughter who was in high school, and me. It was a perfect picture of yesterday, today, and tomorrow! Certainly the conversation bore that out. Susan was reporting to Mother and me about one of her classes. The general heading was "Social Problems," the specific subject that day had been abortion, and the indication was that it had been a no-holds-barred discussion. Mother was shocked to discover that "these things" were a matter of public education, and horrified to learn that Susan's class was a coed one!

Seeing the picture in my mind's eye still makes me laugh. Sue was her natural intense self, perfectly at ease. Mother tried to control her giggling born of nervousness, and I was giving a stellar performance of outward, casual calmness! It's been written about extensively as the generation gap.

I love being in the middle! There are some advantages in being 50-some, albeit there are those who say you must be 70 to know what they are. I'm old enough to remember and relish the good old days and young enough to appreciate the marvels of these good *new* days! And I have great hopes and expectations for the good days just ahead.

Some of the things I remember, however, from the good old days are very strange to today's child. For instance, I remember a world with*out* pizza, or McDonalds, or pantyhose, *or* television. Unthinkable! Strange, too, is some of the vernacular of my childhood. "Eating out" then meant taking sandwiches to the backyard, and "gay" meant including streamers and balloons. The "pill" was the kid down the block who pestered all the girls. And the games people played were not psychological, they were "Mother, May I?" "Kick the Can," and "Annie, Annie Over!" These days I laugh to see the clothes of that day coming back as "fashion." Today's designers would not understand, I guess, that we wore them simply because decent girls *never* exposed their ears, elbows, or knees!

I wonder if Whistler's mother did anything besides sit in a rocker? Of course, I am being foolish; yesteryear's women worked very hard. (Thank You, Lord, for an age of gadgets and buttons to push!) But whatever she did, it would pale in the light of her 20th-century counterpart. Let me paint the modern-day version. If you can believe what you hear and read, she is a gorgeous, well-proportioned size 7 who has a Ph.D. Since jogging five miles in the dawn's early light, she has just enjoyed a very productive day in the work force, has changed from the correctly accessorized linen suit into the at-home luxurious silk gown (all made by her) that she now wears as she sits in the living room of an immaculately kept house, reading educationally approved material to her child while the gourmet dinner she has prepared simmers in the oven having been put there immediately after the dining table was set with china, crystal, candles, and fresh flowers. She is also having a nervous breakdown! At least, I *hope* she is. Sure would help *my* self-image!

Yes, we really have come a long way, baby. But in our rolling along, we *have* gathered some moss. Some stubborn problems have attached themselves to our progress like leeches and insist on hanging in there. Some things just have to be in on the action!

It isn't that society hasn't tried to help us all make the transition. There have been tons and tons of material printed, pictured, and preached in various and sundry ways supposedly creating for us the ideal woman . . . *the* female profile! We have been explored, explained, and exploited until sometimes I wonder if we are animal, vegetable, or mineral. Or none of the above!

With the possible exceptions of *Popular Mechanics* and *Burpee's Seed Catalog* one would find it difficult to pick up a magazine void of at least one article telling us how to get it all together. Just yesterday I experimented with that thought at the supermarket. My time did not allow for a thorough survey, but, without exception, every magazine cover my eyes turned to promised to enlighten me on "how to," "what to," "when to," "why I should," and "why I have." All directed to women! The titles offered me ways to slim down, shape up, get around, come across, and work through.

But give us credit! This has been possible because women *do* want to improve. We *do* respond to the challenge of understanding female behavior and reasoning.

Christian women in particular are precious examples! We are not afraid, by and large, to couple psychological makeup with Christian principle, because we know they are not conflicting! They are married . . . united because Christ not only created this intricate machine called woman, but He *is* the foundation and essence of our physical nature as well. We are created in His image, and He stands ready to reveal us to ourselves. My mother had no idea that she needed an understanding of self-actualization, but she sure knew that God knew her needs and could be depended upon to meet them! Faith is still that simple, but the modern forces attacking it are formidable.

Confusion has come, I'm afraid, in trying to solve the paradox of today's demand for a self-sufficient, self-reliant, fulfilled woman and what we perceive as the biblical creature who is spoken of as modest, submissive (such an overworked word!), and a helpmeet. God wants me to lose myself in His will and Spirit; His Word teaches that I must not indulge in self or afford the luxury of self-centeredness, yet I am innately made to need approval and affirmation, and am commanded to love myself!

Add to this the *tremendous* pressure exerted on us constantly to be attractive, sensual, sexual, with it, an equal capable of supporting the family financially as well as emotionally and physically. More than a few have simply not wanted all that thrown at them. I've listened to *so* many who have tried to wade through all the propaganda and still ask themselves, and me, where they fit in. It isn't as simple as browsing through a photo album and saying, "I'll take that one!" Today's woman cannot just window shop, bargain hunt, and cut corners when it comes to identity.

We inevitably come full circle to the realization that whether our career is in the home or the office, or neither, we must accept the fact that there is no escaping the forces besetting us at every level. Never forget, the forces are there. And never forget, as well, they are just as much at work in one locale as another. It is nonsense to entertain the thought that the woman who chooses or can afford to stay in the home does not have very real pressures too.

God would not have us take ourselves out of the world. Neither will He do it for us. Instead, as a part of living He has given to me the responsibility to discover the truth about the one and only person He has given me *total* accountability for: me, myself, and I.

The starting gate for accomplishing this is found in our background. Elementary, my dear Watson! (Every writer is afforded one trite thought!) Is there *anyone* who can fathom the depth of influence background has? Breathes there a therapist or counselor anywhere who dares neglect background? Just as surely as we are what we eat, we are *now* products of where we have been.

"The greatest influence on a child begins with the birth of his parents." I found that quotation tucked inside a banquet program one evening. It was not attributed to an author, but it was surely written by someone with great insight!

Recently a speaker addressing one of the large corporations in our city spoke at length concerning the enormous impact past time periods have on our present outlook. He stressed that what you are NOW is where you were WHEN. For instance, if you are now in the age range of 60, you are probably a very patriotic person and have strong feelings about God and country; but if you are 35-ish, you are more apt to be cynical about such things. If you lived through the great depression or its aftermath, you look at the economy with wary eyes and put a premium on a dollar saved. On the other hand, if you are a child of the credit card age, your concept of money and "things" is influenced a great deal by convenience.

Some of what we are because of background is unchangeable. Princeton University published some very pertinent results of a survey done with 100 women. The participants were the same group surveyed periodically over a 40-year period. One of the important conclusions interested me very much: barring a mental dysfunction, what one is at 30, one will be at 70. There *are* some unchangeables. An outgoing woman of 30 who found interests outside her home and family was outgoing and busy at 70. Those whose scope of activity failed to reach beyond husband, children, and home at 30 were lost for stimulation at 70!

At the time, I was witnessing that truth before my very eyes. My own mother, who at 30 was thrilled to be a dedicated wife, extra-attentive mother, and all-around terrific housekeeper with no other need or desire for expression, could not, at 70, be motivated to break the syndrome and find interest in other areas. Naturally, since husband, children, and home were no longer there, days stretched much longer than 24 hours.

Surely we have all observed that each of us has basic personality traits that do not change. I will always be sanguine! That's a new word I discovered in a crossword puzzle. It means optimistic! That was given to me by my father. He always saw "possibility" and believed unshakably that "this, too, shall pass." I also love to have fun. My mother never outgrew being a cutup. Both of my parents had a marvelous sense of humor, and I like to think mine will never change. If you think our household must have been full of laughter, you're right!

Honesty dictates that I mention at least one undesirable. I am stubborn. I mean the kind of stubborness *not* associated with valiant, noble "causes." That is an inherited liability. I think I stole a little of that from each parent!

Don and I had gone to visit a friend of ours who was residing in a senior citizen's home. Unable to care for herself, she was comfortably adjusting to a house full of people of her same age and problems. Her friends gathered in the sitting room to meet her preacher. She was proud of him and refused to let us leave until he sang for the group. All the time he was doing so one tiny lady watched him with great intensity.

"What nationality are you?" she asked when he had finished.

"Scotch and Irish," he replied.

As quickly as the proverbial wink she said, "Oh, stingy and stubborn, eh?"

We *do* have certain amounts of inherited qualities given to us in the bloodline, so to speak, transmitted to us by the nationality genes.

BUT . . . HOWEVER . . . we have become masters at using the concept of *un*changeable background influence as a cop-out!

>"I am what I am."
>
>"God knows me, that's enough."
>
>"God knows my real intent."
>
>"People just have to take me as I am." (Usually said because we are unable or unwilling to face up to a negative personality trait.)

More importantly, and the greater truth than all I have just said, is the fact that a large part of us *can* be and *is* always and ever changing! If we are willing to look reality square in the face, we *will* grow . . . a process impossible to achieve without change. Every demonstration of growth in the universe is evidenced by change!

Background cannot be blamed for ever and ever, because yesterday, sooner or later, becomes today. And those who never learn to evaluate yesterday's influence for what it is— *forceful* but *limited*—and who cannot break the bonds it imposes, will remain infants in thought and expectation.

We do not ignore background. We could not if we wanted to. We learn to love it, appreciate it, accept it, and when necessary, hold it at arm's length. Best of all is the opportunity to *learn* from it.

It is no exaggeration to say I have spent enough hours to equal several days listening to a very promising young lady who seems to have the ability to make me laugh, cry, sympathize, and agonize all in the same conversation. What sorrows she has suffered! There is no denying that. I am never quite sure what new experience I am going to hear about, but I *am* sure that all the ills of her life are her parents' fault. That is what I will be *told!*

I had known her parents and knew better, but one night I said to her, "Just suppose for agreement's sake that everything you say is true. Your parents were terrible. They have not shown one iota of good sense in raising you. You have suffered immeasurably at their hands. But you are past the age of being 'grown' and now that you have faced the issue squarely and seen it, you can no longer blame their inadequacies for your actions. You have ceased to be under their influence. You have removed yourself from their proximity. *You* must take yourself by the nape of the neck and assume responsibility for yourself and your present actions. As of this very day, the monkey is on your back!"

It is not my intention to delve deeply into the psychological ramifications of prominent malfunctions stemming from background. I do not have the credentials to do so. How I respect those who do! And I urge those who cannot find peace on their own in this area to quickly seek professional aid in understanding. The availability of such help and the absence of the stigma once associated with seeking that help is one of the wonderful, great differences between those good old days and these good new ones!

I would, however, like to mention some common struggles traceable to the past that frequently recur in conversations I have with distressed people. I include them because each time I have addressed myself to them in a group setting, the collective response has greatly affirmed their prevalence and lasting effects.

1. *Instilled inadequacy.* You probably know someone who lives his life expecting failure. I have met so many who see themselves as hopelessly clumsy. Any positive results of their efforts are "mistakes." They do not finish projects. Their mental computers have been programmed with such things as:

> "Can't you do anything right?"
> "I knew you wouldn't do it right!"
> "*Anyone* should be able to understand that."
> "*Why* are you so stupid (or dumb)?"
> "When I was your age, I could do twice as much."

20

These are not necessarily people without love in their background. Many times, just the opposite is true. Children are confronted with their limitations as parents declare, "We love you too much not to tell you."

Jill is a friend of mine whose activity was monotonously scheduled to "just what she could handle." Unnecessary conversation was not included. She had been convinced that everything she might say would be stupid.

After much coaxing she learned to relax with me and express herself freely. What a delightful conversationalist she can be! For months I prodded her to initiate conversation and asked her to simply be interested in what other people had to say. A whole world of expression opened up to her. Consequently, several have sought me out to tell me what an interesting person they have found her to be.

2. *Bondage to a strong parent.* Nothing compares with the sadness one feels for an adult who is incapable of making a decision. Also to be pitied is the one who bears the conviction that he is not *worthy* to decide or act on his own. My heart goes out to those to whom I have listened who cannot find the courage to express an opinion because they fear being *sure* about anything.

> "I will decide what is best for you."
> "You cannot possibly understand the situation. I do."
> "What I say is final; we do not have to discuss it."
> "Surely you would not want to disappoint me."

Dependence upon a parent is disguised many times by the compulsion to extreme measures to prove one's *in*dependence. Some young people, and some not so young, find themselves moving from place to place trying to force distance to break the pattern.

I made the acquaintance recently of a very capable middleaged lady who made me cry with both sadness and joy as she told me of her newfound freedom from the necessity of consulting her mother about every decision and action.

"After putting great distance between us and spending many hours in therapy," she said, "I still fight the urge to pick up the phone to ask her opinion and subsequent approval of my decisions. It is instinctive!"

Her mental surgery has been very painful. She is still in recovery, but she will be well!

3. *Parental discord.* Inferiority wears many faces. One of its masks hides a countenance of fear; emotional fright is often the consequence of excessive disagreement in the home. Fighting, with its various degrees of shouting and yelling, appears to be the only solution to friction and/or frustration. Children assume their home is unusual and different.

Psychologists have discovered in recent years that a great percentage of children of divorced parents feel some measure of responsibility for that divorce, in part because of the child's belief that he has caused the displayed fighting. This is especially true of young children.

Not only are offspring too often unconsenting witnesses to parental conflict, but they are, in many different ways, forced to take sides. Even when there is no understanding of the problem they now discover that, somehow or other, they are participants.

The child of a discordant home oftentimes takes with him to adulthood the identical method for coping. But a host of these children simply find withdrawal as an alternative. Supposedly, silence cannot provoke. Individuality is lost and confined in the prison of "peace at any cost." Some adults will forego any and all personal contribution because they dare not risk conflict.

4. *Constant manipulation to make a child conform.* All parents at some time or other form ideas about the future of their children. We have visions, dreams, ideals for them—as well

we should. We must not, however, manipulate another individual to fit a mold.

The rebellion in a child can be severe enough to result in a downright hatred of those involved. That is extreme. Less extreme, but just as objectionable, are those who live with an underlying, sometimes seething, resentment of suggestions or directions. The adamant, resolute "I'll do it my way!" is not only the cry of one seeking identity but also can be a deliberate declaration of war!

One of my executive friends (a woman) is determined to be a success in her chosen field. I honestly am not sure she enjoys her line of work. I *am* sure, though, that the fact that her parents disapproved of her choice and insisted on something else for her is part of her driving force.

When an occupation is chosen because of parental preference, many adults live long years going through the motions of self-acceptance. They cannot surface above the fixed necessity to please.

5. *Continual comparison to other children.* What far-reaching consequences parents set in motion when they fail to discover identifying traits in each offspring they produce. A child's mind often bypasses the cause and detours to the effect, resulting in a misplaced resentment toward the object of the comparison. Siblings grow to adulthood angry with a brother or sister for possessing a quality so praised by a parent or parents, when in reality the parent has been the neglectful, discriminating agent.

A dear friend confided to me that the reason she had deliberately had but one child stemmed from personal experience in her immediate family. She feared she would not be able to love a second child equally.

"Why can't you be like other children (or so and so)?" (Meaning *better* ones!)

23

"My first child was an angel. This one will drive me crazy!"

"If Jim could only be half as smart as Jane."

One of my own experiences along this line amuses me. My mother equated plumpness with being healthy. She worried about my skinny body and said repeatedly, "I wish you were healthy like Edith," Edith being our neighbor's round daughter. I was embarrassed by my skinniness. It's taken me several years, and Mother is now in heaven, but I would like her to know that I have made it. I am like Edith!

6. *Expected behavior of the opposite sex.* Some parents provide to listening children the conclusion that the opposite sex has special traits reserved just for "their kind." Adults sometimes subtly imply that some emotions, some reactions, some behavior are reserved for male or female.

"Don't try to reason with your mother!"
"Women don't ever know what they want."
"Don't argue with your father. Men have to be right."

There is a move in education to eliminate the stereotypes presented to children in early reading books. Funny, I don't recall concluding just from first grade readers that only women kept house and only men went to work, yet I see how that could happen. I do remember thinking that women cannot be understood because I heard many adult men say so. Sorry, men, but using that cliché sometimes is only an admission that you don't want to deal with the subject at hand. But fair is fair, so down with, "That's just like a man!"

Shame on every mother who has taught her daughter that "this" is standard male behavior and that every male can be expected to do this or that. Every bride and groom who stands to say "I do" has preconceived ideas of what is expected behavior of the other sex. Some are healthy, accurate assessments and some are not. Some of these ideas are so deeply engrained that they are impossible to remove and leave ugly scars in the attempt.

I love listening to a radio commercial I hear often while in my car. Two very young children, a girl and a boy, have taken several rolls of film. The punch line goes something like this:

> Jeffrey: "And you can have them developed at ————'s in such a short time, no matter if they are of birds, or houses, or pets, or of the opposite sex."
>
> Susie: "Jeffrey, are *you* the opposite sex, or am *I*?"

7. *The undisciplined child.* Though other background patterns may appear superficially to have deeper, more far-reaching consequences, I believe this one is the most potentially dangerous. For, while the undisciplined person may find that recognizing negative habits from the growing up years is one thing, changing them is quite another. The very nature of the problem *IS* the problem.

Child abuse is a horrible, frightening thing. But discipline is not abuse. The opposite is true. A child who is not made to appreciate authority and has no acquaintance with discipline *is* abused.

The Bible, in the Book of Proverbs, gives us two very forceful insights into the power and importance of discipline. Found in the 18th verse of chapter 19 are these words: "Discipline your son, for in that there is hope; do not be a willing party to his death." Discipline embraces hope. For what? Life! Not to discipline forecasts a form of death. Many adults are dead to motivation, dead to creativity, and dead to lasting relationships because they have never experienced a regimen of any kind. A child who has never been made to mind grows up fighting the necessity to "mind" his own drives and instincts. Those around him behold the results: a chaotic and unorganized mind and life.

Second, the whole matter of discipline is soldered to self-esteem. In Prov. 15:32, we encounter very strong words.

"He who ignores discipline despises himself, but whoever heeds correction gains understanding." It is impossible to determine if the one ignoring discipline is the overseer or the overseen, but the truth aptly applies to both. Those who refuse to discipline and the victims of that form of abuse both bear the seed of self-hate and find that to do as one pleases ultimately cancels freedom. Alas, some never learn that lesson.

This brings us to the end of my enumerated list. I do want to add a word about one other, that of child molestation. Sociologists tell us it is not new by any means, just newly acknowledged. These instances are too delicate to detail.

Many years ago I heard for my first time one such story. I was camp "Ma." Cindy was a loner, a frightened teenager who found something in my smile that gave her the courage to knock on my door in the middle of the night. There, huddled in the hallway, she trusted me with her life.

In the intervening years I have not found the ability to fathom such behavior. But I have worked and watched to see God heal the unhealable emotions, to witness the transformation from worthlessness to forgiveness and esteem! The victim of the most complex story I've ever heard has experienced the most miraculous change of all. God has healed her mind and emotions as surely as He made the blind to see! The P.S. is "Praise the Lord!"

Have these pages brought a definition to some reflection in *your* mirror? Do you need a formula for help? Healthy self-image demands, insists, upon action. God expects it. Today deserves it!

What can you do to start right now?

First of all, make two lists. I hate lists! Mainly because I subconsciously react to the premise that I cannot remember everything I should. I can't, either. But there is a beneficial time and place for lists. This is one of them.

The first list is very simple—maybe! It will have two columns:

| The good gleaned from my background | How I use this strength now |
|---|---|
| | |

Beneath the left heading list the positive forces in your present life stemming from your background. These may be material things, qualities of spirit, viewpoints, spiritual concepts, or physical attributes. Pray about each entry as you complete the right-hand column. You may discover some very positive characteristics you have neglected to put to use!

The second list will have four columns:

| Undesirable aspects from background | How this is reflected in my life today | Others presently affected | A scripture I claim for this |
|---|---|---|---|
| | | | |

In addition to those in the first list, the second should include prejudices, habits, moods, and attitudes. Don't keep any secrets! You may want to take several days to complete the exercise, for no one day will bring you face-to-face with the entire list. And it may take given situations or circumstances to reveal how others around you are affected by your behavior.

Search diligently through your favorite Bible translation and find a scripture or passage you can claim as your very own concerning each item listed. Read it daily. Learn to live by it and with it!

Destroy bitterness at any cost! This is the truest of truth: Bitterness is the boa constrictor of personality! It is the death knell of joy and the executioner of peace. Bitterness will kill! Its prey, however, *is not the thing or person that is its cause;* its victim is the one who harbors and hides the hurt, the injustice and its consequence, and cosmeticizes the scar.

The apostle Paul prescribed the perfect antidote to bitterness when he fervently vowed to the Corinthians, "We work hard with our own hands. When we are cursed, we bless; when we are persecuted, we endure it; when we are slandered, we answer kindly" (1 Cor. 4:12-13).

A man named Job was bullish about bitterness. Job suspected he had troubles. When his three friends showed up to "sympathize with him and comfort him," he was sure of it! Bildad, the Shuhite, in his "helping" proclaimed to Job (among other things) that God did not count Job as righteous, for man, who is only a worm, cannot be righteous before God. Job's "friend" opened wide the door of opportunity for Job to fellowship with bitterness. After all, hadn't he been faithful through all this mess? God would dare deny Job's righeousness? Why doesn't God *do* something? Ah, Job's resolve *was* God doing something. Listen:

> As surely as God lives, who has denied me justice, the Almighty, who has made me taste bitterness of soul, as long as I have life within me, the breath of God in my nostrils, my lips will not speak wickedness, and my tongue will utter no deceit. I will never admit you [Bildad] are in the right; till I die, I will not deny my integrity. I will maintain my righteousness and never let go of it; my conscience will not reproach me as long as I live *(Job 27:1-6).*

28

The solution to bitterness is basically one step! Release it! Let it go! Accept the limitations on setting the record straight. You may need professional assistance in doing that. You probably will need to exercise severe mental determination. You certainly will need God's help and healing. Rejoice! It can be done!

Exhibit A stood before me just the other day declaring almost gleefully, "I have done all that I can do. I have let go of it! I have released it and I am FREE! If someday God writes another ending, I shall be grateful. But the bitterness shall not have to be dealt with again. He has melted it away with His healing!"

The Bible specifically declares that love records no wrong. If for an instant you impulsively feel a need to record the hurt, write it in sand! The high tide of God's patience will wash it away, or the wind of His Spirit will obliterate its message!

Consider these lines found in Margery Wilson's book *The Woman You Want to Be.* "Anything, great or small, that causes you to want to draw down the blinds . . . is extremely damaging to your peace of mind and therefore to your charm. . . . Nothing can do you lasting harm *except as you hug it mentally and demand that it remain with you.*"[1]

Decide today to eliminate the word *blame* from your vocabulary as it pertains to background. This present day, the *now* of your life, is served no good whatsoever by reaching into yesterday to establish blame. And it makes no difference how distant or recent that yesterday may be.

You may be entirely right. The blame may rightfully belong to someone else. Blaming this day's progress or outcome on the actions or influences of the past may seem to lighten the load for you, but in reality it will add a burden to the

---

1. Margery Wilson, *The Woman You Want to Be* (Philadelphia: J. B. Lippincott Co., 1942, 1970), 152.

beauty and possibility of *this* day. True, *this* is the day the Lord hath made! He made it—THIS one—just for you, and He has a special road for you to walk. Don't take a side street!

Charles Swindoll's book *Hand Me Another Brick* contains this insight: "When you cast blame and criticism you squelch motivation. When you identify with the problem, you encourage motivation."[2]

Isn't it just possible that to allow ourselves to escape into the luxury of blaming yesterday for today we water the habit of rationalization and make way for a giant harvest of excuses?

---

2. Charles R. Swindoll, *Hand Me Another Brick* (New York: Bantam Books, Inc., © 1981), 40.

# 2

# Reflected Distortions

CERTAINLY there are many, many people who have enjoyed healthy and memorable childhoods. I have met and listened to examples from all ages who remember the past as "Daddy loved Mommy, Mommy loved Daddy, and they both loved me." They sincerely meant it! In fact, my own background was very much like that. I still have a tendency to admit only to happiness, rosiness, and a "tiptoeing through the tulips." Our home was not only motherhood and apple pie but also peanut butter cookies, with lots and lots of security served in between. My mirror seldom reflected anything other than pleasantness.

Those of us who come to adulthood this way are somewhat naive and really very vulnerable. That, in part, explains our susceptibility to pressures that are meaningless to others. Nonetheless, not one of us is invincible. A very popular song declares that because "I am woman, I am invincible." Don't you believe it! That may make a fine theme song, but it is idealistic and dangerous.

All of us have probably walked through the fun house and laughed at ourselves in the assortment of distorted mirrors found there. My grandchildren on a recent outing had great fun seeing me seven feet tall, four feet wide, and with measurements of 50-22-50! I wouldn't suggest that the distorted mirrors of our lives are as extreme, but often they reflect an unnatural, abnormal likeness.

This is true at times because of background, sometimes not. But the little distortions *are* there, and even though we cannot always blot out their cause, we *can* clean off the surface to see a prettier picture.

Rejection, the lack of affirmation in our lives, experiences of humiliation and feelings of inferiority, and the residue of failure all leave fingerprints. Once in a while they steam up the whole surface, and we cannot see a likeness at all! Let's look!

## Rejection

"Now, Lord, please do me one very big favor! Please take time out from rescuing humans from themselves, and write a dissertation for me explaining *exactly* how you feel about divorce! So many people have so many ideas, I just want your version scribbled on a couple of tablets by you personally. Oh, you did that already? Well, then, I have a small questionnaire for you. How come some of the nicest people in the world are divorced? What happens, Lord, to two people who say they know You personally and yet can't make it with each other? How can people walk in and out of commitment so quickly? Lord, is the grass really greener on the other side of the fence? Just where is the healing salve for all the broken homes and hearts? Is it still on the ark? Then let someone find the ark soon! And here's a baffling one: why don't You YELL LOUDER at some of Your children who can't seem to hear Your soft voice saying not to marry that one in the first place? More immediately, I need to know how to minister to some very sweet people who have tried and tried to shed rejection. Some of them, Lord, can hardly look themselves in the mirror. Lord, please heal rejection."

Please believe me, the above is not meant to be flippant or amusing. There is nothing funny about divorce. I do not know experientially, but I know by observation that there is no easy answer for healing the hurt, for regaining self-worth, or for facing the world's various reactions even in a liberated society.

Over the years my husband and I have watched as couples have divorced for every conceivable reason. I believe we have seen and heard it all. I liken it to improvisation in music: variations on a theme!

The reasons run the gamut from valid, heartrending causes to flimsy, irrational excuses. Atmosphere varies from hostile hatred to "let's be friends through it all." But always there is one sure ingredient: hurt people. Hurt sits on a foundation of rejection, and Satan has a heyday bouncing the emotions of hurt and rejection against the wall of stigma and misunderstanding, and flinging continual reminders back in the face.

Judy had not had exposure to the gospel, but she recognized the downhill course her marriage was taking. She turned to the church seeking answers. She was unable to stem the tide and salvage her marriage, but she did find the Savior! She became very involved with Christian friends, working alongside many of them in the church. They prayed for her. They encouraged her, and she grew rapidly. It was soon evident, however, that the bills were going to be more than she could handle, and she found it necessary to move out of state to be near family and home.

She visited several churches. Settling on the one nearest her made good sense, and she attended several services. Sorry to say, she left as lonely as when she had arrived, and she began to look elsewhere.

One day someone from the nearby church missed her. A call was made. Judy was not overly responsive.

"Why aren't you coming back to church?" the caller asked.

My friend tried to be tactfully honest.

"Well, I tried to feel comfortable, but no one really was friendly to me."

No hesitation on the caller's part: "That," she said, "is because you are divorced."

Stigma. Rejection.

"Lord, why do we reject those whose steps have taken them (for whatever reason) down paths foreign to us? Why do we need to deny the existence of the wilderness or the jungle just because we haven't been there?"

My motive is not to be hard on the church—any church! The world, too, has its own methods of cruelty, some of them far more subtle in their discrimination. Nor would I even hint that divorce be made more acceptable or natural. My plea, rather, is that we in the church do everything in our power (and we profess access to the greatest power in the world) to peel away the layers of disappointment, fear, and rejection, and replace them with love, gentleness, and acceptance. *We have acceptance and approval so mixed up!*

Divorce, in its prevalence, surely must have great store-houses for the amounts of rejection it produces. Divorce *is* rejection. There is no escaping it, I suppose. Even in instances where two people are really better off without each other (and our refusal to acknowledge that kind of condition does not negate its reality), there is still deeply felt rejection when divorce occurs. Rejection also plagues those who decide they no longer care for each other or can convince themselves that they never did.

I admit I do not understand the popularity of the living-together arrangement. I am confused by its justification and shocked at some I have known so well who have chosen to do so. Neither do I, however, understand the sorrow and sympathy I feel. I wish I could just say, "Well, it's their lives." Why does my heart ache so? Permit me to partially answer my own question.

It is hard to dismiss the sadness and hurt and rejection I see on faces of those who sit across from me at coffee and talk of what remains of the disillusionment. For my sensitive friends, the pill of exploitation is a hard one to swallow. Laying all moral standards aside, as many do so easily, I object to the whole scenario because I have yet to meet a girl or woman who escapes without a damaged self-esteem!

One of the prettiest girls I know is also one of the most lovable. She has a beautiful smile seldom seen. She finds it difficult to keep a job simply because she is convinced she is not worth a salary. She has lived with several male partners, all of whom have eventually walked away from the relationship. The reasoning computer of her mind constantly confirms her worthlessness. How she would love to be a Christian. "But God, too, is male, and He will reject me also."

John Kennedy said, "We have nothing to fear but fear itself." (Franklin Roosevelt said it first.) Rejection is like that. We feel rejected because we *fear* rejection. If only we could know the intent of all the others in our sphere of activity, we would be less fearful. Of course, we cannot. What we can do for ourselves at this point is to discipline the mind. I will not dwell on or imagine the motives of others or their opinions of me. I cannot read other minds, nor can I always be a good judge of the meaning behind someone else's words or actions.

That brings to mind one other culprit: our multiplied insecurities. We all have insecurities; therefore, to some degree, we all feel rejection. Insecurity operates on a scale from those who interpret *any* disagreement with them as rejection, to those who seemingly are incapable of having their feelings hurt at all.

This is important: Few of us are rejected purely on the basis of our person. Rejection, more often than not, is based on another's perception of our circumstances, intelligence, social status, what we can do for them, etc. If we could only see that! When that is the case, it is *their* problem!

*If* we have done our best in the Lord to maintain His approved standard of conduct (love, joy, peace, kindness, gentleness, etc.), rejection should then be regarded as the "rejector's" problem. We have no right to be brazen, but we do well to remind ourselves that we cannot *force* feeling or emotion or even acceptance from others. How often have I observed the distortion of an otherwise lovely personality, brought about by an attempt to prevent his own rejection!

God has great help for us. He is very well acquainted with rejection. In today's language, "He knows the territory!"

> For the Son of Man . . . must suffer many things and be rejected by this generation *(Luke 17:24-25)*.

> Blessed are you when people insult you, persecute you and falsely say all kinds of evil against you because of me. Rejoice and be glad, because great is your reward in heaven, for in the same way they persecuted the prophets who were before you *(Matt. 5:11)*.

> Because you love me, I will rescue you; I will protect you, for you acknowledge my name. You may call on me, and I will answer you; I will be with you in trouble, I will deliver you and honor you *(Ps. 91:14-15, author's paraphrase)*.

> Ye are the temple of the living God; as God hath said, I will dwell in them, and walk in them; and I will be their God, and they shall be my people *(2 Cor. 6:16, KJV)*.

> The Lord thy God turned the curse into a blessing unto thee, because the Lord thy God loved thee *(Deut. 23:5, KJV)*.

God waits. God responds!

If this were a coupon, I would say of the following: "Clip and Save!" It is profound:

> He who draws nigh to God *one inch* through doubting dim,
> God will advance one mile in blazing light to him!
> —Author unknown

## Lack of Affirmation

It pays to advertise. It really must be true. Everybody is trying to sell me something, making profit the creator of billions of words and pictures that intrude upon my life whether I give permission or not. Mind and activity are constantly bombarded with attention-getting phrases and jingles designed to convince me that a product not only is exactly what I need but also was *invented* just for me! I should be so gullible! Amusing, isn't it, that the state of my day and well-being is such a concern to the solicitor until I say, "No, thank you"?

We live in an age when not just products and services are marketed, but causes and philosophies, too. Nor is advertisement limited to the traditional media. Plain brown bags do not exist at my supermarket. My groceries are put into my car clothed in brown paper printed with various messages and admonitions for me to read as I unsack my purchases at home.

Plaques, posters, and billboards talk to me all day long. And several times I have lost my concentration in traffic trying to catch the ditty on a bumper sticker. Can you believe I "communicate" with signs and stickers? Sometimes I talk back:

"Have you hugged your kids today?" *I would if I could get out of this traffic!*

"Smile, God loves you." *Thank goodness someone does today.*

"This car brakes for garage sales." *Where? Where?*

"A well-kept house is the sign of a misspent life!" *Right on! Far be it from me to waste time!*

"It does no good to talk about dieting, you must keep your mouth shut." *Alas, I'm all talk!*

The world is bulging with words! Words and more words. Is there any reason that anyone should feel alone and unworthy? No. But he, she, they, you, and I all do at times! Communication is so available, but so elusive. So uninterested a lot of the time. People walk in and out of each other's lives as easily as walking full circle through a revolving door, scarcely aware of anything other than their own praises and problems.

Unfortunately, for many, many people, the mirror of the soul reflects badly distorted pictures of the self because the beauty of that self has been marred by a lack of affirmation. No one gives them "strokes." The approval and assurance given to another in recognition of positive qualities, assets, or actions is lacking. The inner self starves, hungry to be fed a morsel of acclamation. Satan is elated! Even though he knows from firsthand conversation that "man does not live on bread alone, but on every word that comes from the mouth of God," he knows all too well that malnutrition of the spirit of man slowly overpowers self-worth and saps from the individual the incentive to appropriate God's Word. The ego concludes that surely since no one else thinks I have worth, ability, a contribution to make, it must be so!

Remember the appearance a few years ago of a book that rapidly became a best-seller, titled *I'm O.K., You're O.K.* The title was worth the price! How great to have someone, even a stranger, affirm that I have redeeming qualities! Millions of people responded to the pat on the back that spoke hope and worthiness.

All of us have to have affirmation. A child barely puts one foot ahead of the other before he looks expectantly for the nod of approval or the delighted squeals of adulation. The human heart will die, figuratively and literally, if left solely to its own imagination for self-worth. It will not only shrink to a very small bundle of unworthiness, neatly wrapped and tied by neglect, but it will suffer physically, being unable to breathe midst the heaviness of self-pity.

Some try to escape the perils of a sense of worthlessness by creating and affirming their own positive evaluation of themselves. But it isn't the same. Nothing replaces or substitutes for acclaim, no matter how small, given by another human being.

Is there a more graphic demonstration of "going in circles" than the self-acclaimed egotist who lauds his own attributes in the attempt to flee his prison cell of loneliness? He has been exiled to his own island of exaggerated self-image because no one in his life has rescued him from himself by sincere affirmation. Not one stroke!

My dear friend, Mabel, and I were entering a restaurant recently. I hadn't seen her for a while and she surprised me by her new behavior.

"My, what a pretty hairdo!" she said.

I knew she wasn't talking to me, for mine was a mess that day. I turned to see a lady leaving, wearing a startled, grateful smile and a pretty hairdo!

I said nothing. Later, on our way to the car my friend spoke again to a stranger.

"That is a lovely dress!" Another startled smile.

"What's with you and all the strangers?" I asked.

"You know," she replied, "I have discovered that so many people have so few compliments given to them that I have decided that whenever I honestly think something nice in passing I am just going to tell that person so. Why not spread a little self-confidence?"

Mabel, guess who is cheering you on? Solomon! He must have known about strokes, for he wrote in the 25th division of Proverbs that "a word aptly spoken is like apples of gold in settings of silver!"

Many years ago I read an amusing real-life story in *Reader's Digest*. A trucker asked a friend to ride with him on a long-distance run. The friend was delighted. But not many miles down the road his delight began to wane. He was shocked to see his friend roll down the window to whistle at a young mother pushing a baby buggy. He was puzzled because the whistling was repeated during the next few days several times, and he thought he knew his friend to be a happily married man.

Finally, after several hundred miles and many small towns, he approached the subject.

"Why the whistling?"

"Oh, nothing personal," the driver assured him. "I just remember how lousy and ugly my wife felt after having a baby. One day a man whistled at her and she recovered her self-esteem! Just thought I'd return the favor."

The Christian finds affirmation in and from Christ! God has declared in so many ways that He puts an unmeasurable premium on your head and mine, not said just by His death and resurrection, but by our very creation. Besides being made in His image, we have dominion over the earth. We are redeemed with a high price, no markdowns or sale tags. Eternity is prepared for *us*. Each of us is worth more individually than the whole world. He said so. God said it and that settles it whether I believe it or not! Then, since it *is* settled, you can believe it! We don't have to ad-lib. He wrote the script!

One more time! The Christian finds affirmation in and from Christ! Sadly, some hang there by the skin of their teeth! I talked to the Lord about that one day. Such a realization disturbed me.

I was walking along a narrow, winding path intermingling my thoughts and steps with the beautiful Colorado mountain scenery engulfing me. I had sought the solace of the mountainside to prepare my heart for a speech I was to give that morning. My week had included long, separate conversations with two struggling persons who really had no affirmation in their lives except what Christ gave through His Word and His presence.

"That isn't *enough!*" I protested to the Lord.

My heart ached in sympathy. He spoke to me very clearly: "Pat, tell them this morning that if my approval is *all* they have, it IS ENOUGH! One of mine who will be there needs to know!"

That affirmation from Christ is often the difference between coping and suicide! One beautiful aspect about God is that He will not leave us clinging to the limb of isolation. The lack of affirmation need not be long lasting. Hang in there! He will send someone from His family to "whistle." Oh, that His family would move more swiftly, be increasingly sensitive to those hanging on to the rope of His assurance! We must be available. "Rope burn" must be minimal!

> Let us hold unswervingly to the hope we profess, for he who promised is faithful. And let us consider how we may spur one another on toward love and good deeds. Let us not give up meeting together, as some are in the habit of doing, but let us encourage one another *(Heb. 10:23-25)*.

## Humiliation and Inferiority

Some mirrors are sold with two sides, one for a conventional reflection, the other for magnification. Down inside the storeroom of self-esteem is one just like that. Occasionally, when I have needed to take a look at a humiliating experience, I have inadvertently chosen the wrong side and the whole ordeal suddenly has blossomed to magnified proportions. What should have been a simple embarrassment has become a lasting, deep-red blush. An upheaval!

The emotions of humiliation and inferiority walk hand in hand. Together they pose a classic "which-came-first-the-chicken-or-the-egg" dilemma. Inferiority marches us headlong into humiliation, and real or imagined feelings of humiliation heap fuel on the burning cinders of inferiority.

Very real things instill inferiority in us. Our finances, or what we feel is lack of fashion sense, may cause us to feel our appearance is inadequate; we may be limited in knowledge; previous mishaps may have convinced us we are clumsy. Putting our foot in our mouth on a regular basis can make us feel inferior and hesitant around people who are very comfortable with conversation.

41

Joyce Landorf speaks of having "balcony people" in our lives, those who pull us up, encourage us, and cheer us on. Thank God! Yet, incredible as it is, some people, usually from out of their own inferiority, heap doses of inferiority and humiliation on others by their constant put downs. And many who have no convenient or knowledgeable way out of the arena must endure them!

A great lady, who is probably unaware of the influence she has been in my life, once said, "No one can make you feel inferior without your permission!" Mrs. V. H. Lewis wrote that on the tablet of my heart. I have mulled it over many, many times and repeated it as often. To the Christian it should have a tremendous impact. Incidentally, handle it with care: it can easily lead to egotism without the safeguard that knowing Christ provides.

Close your eyes and recall a time when you desperately wanted to be at your best. That was the situation I found myself in one night shortly after my husband and I had arrived in a new pastorate. We hadn't been in town long, just long enough for someone to decide that if I gave the study at the monthly missionary meeting this would be a great way for all those present to get to know me.

I walked into one of the most beautiful homes I had ever seen. Its floors were hugged by thick white carpets; its walls were proudly clothed with treasures of art, and its accessories sparkled with shiny marble and gleaming gold leaf. Its owner and hostess was as elegant and lovely as its appointments. My own value system filled me with inferiority.

Preliminary business was taken care of. Cinderella's clock struck 12:00. I rose to begin the study, simultaneously sending a small marble table to its demise. What happened next is almost a complete blank. Thankfully, time has erased my misery. Once my own front door shut behind me, however, I burst into a torrent of tears. My scared husband, thinking someone had died, flew to my side.

"What in the world is the matter?"

I relayed the story with all the dramatics of a Shakespearean tragedy.

He set me down, made me look at him, and said, "What did Rhoda say about it?"

Rhoda! What difference did it make what Rhoda said? I could die! I had forgotten about Rhoda.

"Well, among other things, she laughed at its unimportance. She said that it was the least favorite thing of hers in the whole house, that it was very inexpensive, that she really had planned to get rid of it, and that it wasn't worth 60 seconds' concern."

My tears reduced to trickles. Not one person had imposed humiliation and inferiority on me except myself! To feel bad was appropriate; to die a thousand deaths for days was ridiculous. Thank you, Rhoda, for "letting" me break your table. For that experience has prompted me on many occasions to be sure I am looking into the right side of the mirror. Oh, I must see humiliation and inferiority, but I have no desire or need to magnify the ugly things!

### Failure

Success is never final
>Failure is never fatal
>>It's the courage that counts!

Winston Churchill wrote those words and I'm wondering if they were not the impetus behind his famous V for victory sign? He was best friends with failure, having been in its presence often. We aren't sure just when he concluded that failure need not be fatal, but he exemplified that truth to the world. Perhaps his knowledge of failure was responsible, in part, for his successes having long outlived him.

Actually, there is a very subtle kinship between success and failure. To permit success to become final automatically transfers it to another category, and, in that respect, success becomes fatal! This is not just a play on words: success is failure when it succeeds in being final.

Failure is not a four-letter word, but it is just as distasteful to us. In times of retrospect we are apt to see failure more often than other facets of our lives. It glares at us. Even if we could diminish the magnitude of any given failure, we would still see it in our looking glass.

What is failure? Under *fail* in the dictionary, several descriptions are listed: "to be unable to do or become what is wanted, expected, or attempted; fall short; to neglect; lack." How succinctly put! All activity falls within the scope of that definition: wanted, expected, attempted, and often one incidence of failure encompasses all three.

What a fine line separates deeds of aspiration and attempts of absurdity sometimes! Some failure comes simply because of the inability or refusal to recognize the personal limitations we have.

I get inspired listening to the great motivators who build a wonderful case that I can do *anything* in the world that I want to do. In the final analysis that is absolutely true. However, lots of things have no real "want to" for me. I should recognize this and continually avoid trying to make myself "enjoy" the effort. Reaching out to stretch potential is one thing; cutting the pattern to fit the cloth is quite another. To want to do something for all the wrong reasons is not enough. It will not ultimately be soul satisfying.

Furthermore, painful experiences of the past may cause me to embrace certain limitations, and "wanting to" is not worth the try. This little illustration bears that out.

I needed a summer job. I had just arrived home from college and next year's education was only three months away. I was delighted to be hired in a ladies' apparel shop in the large city adjacent to our small town. I was delighted to have found a job and being able to walk among so many pretty dresses was a fringe benefit!

How I laugh about it now! Since, up to that time, most of my clothes had been made for me, I was not aware that when a customer asked, "How does this look on me?" I should not have said, "Really, not very good," or, "The color is wrong," or, even worse, "Shouldn't you try a size larger?"

The dresses lasted longer than I did.

My father dealt with my ruffled feathers of failure. "You have tested those waters, now try another pond. You'll find one where you can swim!"

I did. But that experience provided me some needed perspective about buying and selling. I'm great at buying, repulsed by selling. If push comes to shove, I would force myself to sell, but *never* could I be made to want to!

All of us, at times, have been captivated by the admonition to reach for the stars. The possibility is inspiring and exhilarating! But defining the stars and their locations is part of the process of reaching them. The spirit of a man may soar to heights unseen by his peers, but that flight is not a success if the spirit soars and soars without pinnings and moorings! The status quo becomes stagnated if we never reach beyond the obvious and easy, but failure is automatic if we do not ever know what it is like to wrap up an endeavor and label it *achieved!*

Perhaps the greatest failure of all is to allow a large percentage of what we do to be dictated by the expectations of others. I am not referring to that empowering element provided by the faith of another in me. Each of us needs that. I refer, instead, to that form of exploitation made up of *imposed* expectation. To some degree, failure follows. Not so much a failure of the outward and visible but that of the inward knowledge that I have failed to stand on my own two feet. To continually acquiesce means I just don't grow up.

Consider a couple of positive lessons learned in failure.

First, there is the decentralization of the person. Failure is one of the best agents for bringing a person to the realization that no man is an island unto himself. Many are multifaceted, 10-talented individuals. Success does not come by talent alone, nor does it thrive only on capability. It has to include some degree of dependence. When failure forces the fall from a pedestal of self-centeredness, great progress *is* available. It is an accomplishment indeed to pick up the broken pieces of egotism and begin anew, decentralized!

Second, failure confirms what we so easily forget: There is a temporal aspect of *all* things. "This, too," shall not only pass, it *is* passing now! Nothing is forever, even failure!

Contemplate this: failure is as necessary to the growth of man's character and spirit as water and air are to his body. How else can I judge success or taste its self-assurance?

Riding along in my car one day I decided to do something that I rarely do, for it is an exercise I usually regard as useless. My mind was embroiled in the throes of a problem. "I'm going to turn on the radio," I said as I adjusted the tuner to a frequency I knew played Christian music. "The first song I hear will be my message from the Lord." Imagine my surprise to hear, "You'll never know what homesick is until you've been away from home." Point well taken! I have paraphrased that thought many times since, just as I am doing here. How will we know what success is all about unless we agonize through failure? Besides, to succeed 100 percent of the time would turn me into a spoiled brat, spiritually. The human spirit cannot bear that kind of onus!

One little caution at this point. God forbid that I should revel in failure. Everything about me as a person stands in danger of dehydration should I become comfortable with failure. Failure must be a learning tool, not a life-style!

Parenthetically, don't fall into the trap of repeated, unsuccessful attempts at the same thing. Maybe the advice of a comedian I once heard is more than comedy: If at first you don't succeed, try something else!

God is very involved with us in failure. Or at least He wants to be. Maybe knowing that humanity would struggle so with failure was what prompted Him to fill His Word with so many examples of it. Failure in its most devastating form is the inability to pick up the pieces. Praise the Lord that the availability of strength to do just that is the message God tacks on to the accounts of failure in His Word!

He shouts to us through Solomon that "though a righteous man falls seven times, he rises again" (Prov. 24:16). In Him are the resources to regroup and rise from the ashes. They are guaranteed to us by the absolute absence of failure in Him. Joshua reminded the Israelites, who were so prone to failure, that they had at their disposal the basis for regrouping and starting over. The bottom line, said he, is that "you know with all your heart and soul that not one of all the good promises the Lord your God gave you has failed. Every promise has been fulfilled; not one has failed" (Josh. 23:14).

**The New Mirror**

Now, here we are. God would have us package up the reflections and let Him take us as we are. He will apply His unequaled know-how in the resurfacing of mirrors to make sure that every reflection *counts*. When we have faced up to the makeup of inner self we are properly prepared to do that.

Let's take a long, hard look at ourselves. We actually have begun already! Share with me two very pertinent passages:

> . . . you have taken off your old self with its practices and have put on the new self, which is being renewed in knowledge in the image of its Creator *(Col. 3:9-10)*.
>
> Whatever you do, work at it with all your heart, as working for the Lord, not for men *(Col. 3:23)*.

47

In Colossians, Paul reasons that now that we have put on the new self (that image of the Creator) we should do whatever we do with all our heart.

He pleads with us in Galatians to do our very best:

> Let everyone be sure that he is doing his very best, for then he will have the personal satisfaction of work well done, and won't need to compare himself with someone else (Gal. 6:4, TLB).

We are ready to hold the mirror in God's direction. There we can and will see *His* face, *and* ourselves, the image of the Creator!

# 3

# Let Everyone Be Sure That He Is Doing His Very Best

PARENTS are not supposed to be smart! Educated is fine, but smart is very difficult for a child to grow up with. And if parents are smart *and* intuitive, as mine were, a child really has a problem! After spending several years watching my older brothers fail in their repeated attempts to fool my father, I learned early not to try it. I don't think I ever did. Succeed, that is!

My father set the rules of our home on precept and principle, and carried them out on instinct! Whether he became convinced that one should do his best while pitching hay, butchering hogs, learning to maneuver one of those 1929 autos, or later while carrying the U.S. mail, I don't know. But it was ingrained in him. I began kindergarten hearing him say, "Just do your best." A snap for me at 5! Easy at 10. A little harder at 15, and more than a little boring at 18.

By then I had heard the admonition applied to about every activity and circumstance imaginable.

"Mother and I just expect you to do your best."

"Fine if you are at the top, but you must be able to say you have done your best."

"I'll not be upset if you are *not* at the top, as long as I know you could not have done better."

"This severe disappointment is really only skin deep for you if inside you can be assured that you have done your best!"

Oh, how clever. Then came the day when I comprehended: My best was *all* I really had to offer anyone, *especially* myself. There certainly are many routes through "good" and "better" before one gets to "best." My father knew intuitively that when I tried to pawn good and better off for best, that there was a restlessness within me that always brought me face-to-face with *me*. And that was his desired end result all along.

At this point, let's make a few observations about the word *best*.

For us to use the word correctly, it must be put on a plane by itself. Any dictionary will define it in relationship to some other word, quality, or standard. Pretty is judged in part in relation to ugly; failure has to include a knowledge of success; and industrious makes sense only if one knows what lazy is.

Furthermore, best is always measurable! But quickly we must accept the fact that best is a quality defined in relation to something else. It cannot, or should not, be always measured by the same stick. I may this day have read the best book I have ever read, but if my reading only extends to two or three books a year, that "best" book better not stand on my appraisal.

Best can seldom be duplicated exactly as we achieved it, because the variables are so changeable. But it *can* be measured!

One of the most difficult attitudes concerning best for us to get through the head is that it is not necessarily the cause of or forerunner to success. If, indeed, we were somehow able to delete from our thinking all those cultural criteria that spell success to us, we could better understand what best is all about, especially as it relates to our Christian development. Success comes easily to some who really have not brought it about by giving of their best. And just as true is the stark realization that on occasion I *know* in my heart I have done my very best and the outward, visible "what-people-see" results have not seemingly been successful.

Best cannot always be mine to give. Now, I know that seems contradictory to the admonition from Galatians. And yet, it *is* always available.

Let me explain. We are seldom, if ever, persons of total autonomy, and sometimes when we have an assignment, or desire to accomplish a given thing, there are people or circumstances who make it impossible for us to carry out our best ideas and efforts. We simply are forced to accept the fact that we cannot work as we would like. Our best is thwarted by something outside our jurisdiction. But best comes . . . is there . . . is mine, when I *graciously accept that the job I could have done is beyond my authority.* My *best* at this point is that inward refusal to accept bitterness, ill-will, or superiority as alternatives and to smile with approval when the end result is less than it could have been.

OK. What is my best? Simply, it is to live up to my potential. What is my potential? The *World Book Dictionary* includes this phrase: "possible as opposed to actual." How do I know what is possible for me? What is actual? The answers lie in how well I know myself. What is myself? And now we come to the exciting part. Or fun part. Or agonizing part as the case may be.

Realizing and recognizing my potential begins at the point at which I take a good, hard look at myself and make the effort to know myself better than I know anyone else in my world.

Oh, dear, I have just conjured up pictures for you of people who are constantly taking their own pulse or who see their therapist twice a day and call *you* in the morning! I chuckle to myself about an acquaintance of mine who has read so much analysis that she has gone through the process of analyzing the analysis many times over and usually ends up back at square one!

Guess what? One of the most wonderful aspects of potential is that it is full of surprises! I still view with surprise some of the assignments I have accepted over the years just because there was no one else to do them, being convinced at the time that I had no proficiency whatsoever (let alone expertise) for that particular job. The surprise was not that I somehow managed to do a reasonably acceptable job but that I actually *enjoyed* the journey!

I am reminded of a well-known television commercial that begins with a lovely young housewife assessing the results of a new appearance created for her. She says, "it is lovely, but it isn't me!" Just once, for reality's sake, wouldn't you love for the lady to say, "I love it! It's an improvement that I like. It *is* me!" You and I both know that some could and would learn to love the new look. And, lo and behold, when I have dared to venture into unexplored potential, I have found many times that this *is* me and God has opened up a whole new arena for *me*.

Our second grandchild was making her first appearance at church. Knowing that grandchild No. 1 might feel suddenly insignificant, I called him and told him that after the service Grandma would have a surprise in her purse. I think he arrived at my side before the "Amen." And so began a tradition! Now, it is Sunday morning blessing for both of us to discover what surprise Grandma might have. I am blessed in the giving, he in the receiving. Do you suppose God is blessed, too, when I accept the opportunity to explore the other side of the open door and, SURPRISE, there is a dimension in my being heretofore latent because I had long since concluded that "That isn't me"?

Everyone who has a sense of humor (and I suspect some who do not) enjoys reading Erma Bombeck. Many of her articles are now classics, including this one that women everywhere can appreciate. After looking Miss Bombeck over while she was browsing at a cosmetic counter in a large department store, the makeup expert offered to "redo" Erma. She consented. The finished product was hardly recognizable to Erma herself. Of course, Erma Bombeck is able to detail a whole column with the transformation, but her point is well made that there is an intangible quality not transformed solely by cosmetics. After changing every visible, outward tint and hue, the saleslady sent her on her way with, "Oh, one more thing, *be yourself!*"

It has been my privilege over the last 27 years to listen to people of all ages, races, and creeds talk about the adventure of knowing themselves. Experience being one of the best teachers, I wish to share the following conclusions with you.

*Knowing oneself is a deliberate, continual process.* There is no escaping that truth, because I am a continually changing substance: physically, emotionally, mentally, and materially. Is there any way to calculate the collective, concerted effort made by humanity to change the process of physical change? We know them well: wrinkling, the natural highlighting of the hair (better known as graying), the loss of elasticity in the muscles, not to mention baldness, or the extra pounds that get more stubborn as the years go by. And, goodness knows, I have not yet ceased to discover emotions in me that were not existent or needed until now. Today may bring emotional disturbance totally foreign and unthinkable yesterday.

Do you remember as a child that very first realization that inside your body lived something that was just *you?* I do. It is one of those things indelibly stamped on my being: there is a ME inside . . . that is only ME . . . unlike any other ME, and it is private and awesome and delicate. I do not remember exactly how old I was, but I shall always remember that confrontation!

Aha! Discovery! The beginning! And now the process.

What a magnificent God who has given me ME and made me in a unique way: one of a kind. Not only do I wish I could erase some of the stagnate intervals along the way from there to here, but I also wish I could pass on one of those money-back guarantees, part and parcel, ready-made, a charted course for those I love. But I can't. It is *mine*.

But I can pass along this proven premise: God intends, yea expects, me to keep an up-to-date, as-best-I-can understanding and acquaintance with myself!

There are at least two reasons why this is so. First of all, Ps. 37:4 begins with the phrase, "Delight *thyself* in the Lord." Genuine self-worth comes only from Christ and only when I see myself in the light of His opinion of me and avail myself to His revelation as to who I really am can I delight *myself* in Him.

Second, if Christianity is anything at all it is internal. If it isn't, it isn't Christianity. If the Bible teaches any tenet at all, it teaches an awareness of the human personality. It admonishes us to develop the fruit of the Spirit, internal attitudes if you will, and constantly prescribes doses of meekness, humility, selflessness, inward peace, and joy. How could God possibly manifest those qualities in my life if I do not mentally acknowledge them, at whatever degree or quantity they do or do not exist in me?

One of the most attitude-changing statements I ever read declared that in the root meaning of the word *humility* is the undeniable truth that to be truly humble one must have a proper evaluation of oneself!

Please don't describe me as crazy now! But I have found great benefit on occasion to remove mentally whatever it is I am frustrated about from my mind and set it in front of me for examination! Most people I know who have a good knowledge of themselves and have achieved the ability to be comfortable with that knowledge have also developed some sort of mental gymnastic, used consistently, to determine who and why they are. When we have no need for the psychologist's couch or therapy group there is great value in a practical, personal self-analysis. A looking into a mirror that no one sees but me.

How long has it been since you have sincerely asked yourself in a quiet moment, Why did I do that? Why did that get to me so, and what is it that gets to me the most? Why do I not accept myself at this point? Why do I need *excessive* attention today? Why do I not like that person? That one is difficult to admit to for many in the Body of Christ.

Note the word *sincere* in the approach. My self-analysis becomes child's play if I am not honestly seeking, or if my motive is merely rationalization. To be nervous about it is an option. Sincerity is a must.

To say that I am a sports nut is like saying water is wet. Of course I am! And I was caught up with the unprecedented excitement in our city of a professional football team that was *winning!* It was an epidemic, a mania, a phobia, all wrapped up in one, and a fire fanned by one winning game after another.

During this season my husband and I were speakers at a conference in a northwestern state. It was Monday night and our team was playing on the network's famous Monday Night Football. I had not been able to see the game, but as we walked to our cabin that night a voice yelled across the grounds that my team was losing.

The next morning I awoke in a decidedly negative mood. Nothing was right. The beautiful sun was really obnoxious in its brightness and I didn't want to face the day. Reason slowly began to prevail. Why do I feel this way? I have done nothing but sleep since everything was great and I was bubbly. I sat down on the bed and made a mental removal of myself from my mind and began to deal with my feelings.

Imagine my utter embarrassment when I came upon the fact that my mood had been determined by the fact that our team was losing a football game! How ridiculous! How degrading! How like me! And how close I had come to losing a magnificent day standing before me with the outstretched hands of new friends and shared spiritual blessing. That day shall always be remembered as a precious one, and I almost missed it!

*Knowing myself must include an understanding of both my strengths and my weaknesses.* A great many people see themselves as leaning toward one or the other. Either their strengths are more obvious to them or their weaknesses are. The well-balanced person is *not* that one who has equal portions of each, but that one who has the ability to recognize and work with the amount of each that he has.

One great weakness that all of us experience some time or another is the failure to see that we can never measure up to what we *think* others expect of us. So then, since we know we cannot make the grade in meeting that expectation, we do nothing. Sometimes we delay doing the significant, waiting for a magic potion that will suddenly make us adequate! What a waste of time.

My husband and I were enjoying a lovely dinner in the home of friends. We had just met some other guests, a couple attending one of our city's seminaries. They both were involved in preparing for the ministry. Since the young man indicated that his course of study was now almost complete, my husband asked if he would be taking a church to pastor soon.

"Oh, no," the young man replied seriously, "my wife has not learned to play the piano yet!"

The young lady's face looked pained. My heart smiled and ached at the same time. What they were doing now was preparing for what they thought *others* would be expecting of them.

Our weaknesses are individually ours. Unfortunately, they seem to come tailor-made!

Dr. Emerson, a noted Christian psychologist, in dealing with a closely related subject, listed one of the five underlying causes of stress as an "excessive awareness of our weaknesses." He cited an experiment done with a class of psychology students whose backgrounds were predominantly Christian. He asked them in five minutes to write their 10 greatest strengths, and in five minutes to list an equal number of weaknesses. Almost without exception the class finished with the asked-for number of weaknesses, but were unable to list their strengths.

Because we have been rightly taught in the church that we must avoid the pitfalls of pride and self-exaltation, we find it very difficult to assess our strengths or to admit our abilities. It is so easy for us to say, "I can't do that." And so difficult to admit, "I can!" Some of the most honest people in the world would be shocked to find that saying they cannot when they really can is not telling the truth!

Likewise, our strengths are individually ours. God has given me *something!* No one is absolutely, totally void of assets. How clear the Bible is at this point. If the talent is one, it is not given lightly; neither is it to be used foolishly. Isn't it a paradox (dealt with in God's Word) that the one who has but one talent has more difficulty dealing with its possibilities than that one who has many? Oh, that all of us could appreciate the greatness of one talent!

Of course, we must deal with both: strength and weakness. When we are not able to see the difference, stress and frustration result. The out-of-balance person has gone to extremes on his perception of one or the other.

Real Christian maturity at this point is to relax in letting God deal with both in us. Matter of fact, He is the only one *qualified* to do so, and the only one who has that right. (Wouldn't it be fun, maybe, to list them for other people?)

So much of negative self-image could be righted here. When God shows me which is strength and which is weakness, my distorted self-image rights itself and progress in knowing myself is amazing.

Amazing, too, is the spiritual phenomenon: When my weakness is objectively recognized and brought to God, He flips the coin over and in my weakness I become strong! Exactly what Paul spoke of when he proclaimed, "When I am weak, then am I strong!"

My weakness, my fault, may be unaltered. In fact, it is spiritual foolishness to believe God transforms all our weaknesses into strengths and makes us persons with all pluses and no minuses. But our ability to cope with our weaknesses is adjusted by God and bathed in His mercy until we can live with it.

The secret of success is to acknowledge my weakness, *know* it, deal with it, improve it. I can name it. And God and I can work with it.

A weakness can be worked with, worked on, and worked out. Over the years there have been times when I felt that my weaknesses needed my best efforts more than my strengths.

Very few people find the first years of marriage to be without adjustments—sometimes petty ones, sometimes serious ones. We were no exception. Surely no one who knew me in those days would believe this, but I could, on occasion, get pretty upset. Putting it honestly, I could lose my temper! Contrary to what one might think, having a mate who had never lost his temper (never has yet that I know of), did not make it easier for me. He didn't understand such behavior!

"That's just the way I am. It's the best I can do."

My line of defense!

I prayed about it. I really did. But I prayed with both ears shut. It was good to pray, and I got better at dealing with it. But I knew in my heart I had not given it my best.

Wonderful day when I owned up to the fact that I was shunning my best effort because I had mistakenly equated an honest willingness to change my weakness with giving in to my mate. And I needed my independence! But enough was enough, and I finally prayed, "O God, I am not at my best either at home or in the ministry. Please give me the courage to deal with this disposition!"

What a revelation! My problem was not one of giving in to my mate or to God, but that of giving in to *me*. I was weak, but I became strong! And free! God and I took a look at *me*. In *His* looking He saw the way to overcome and shared that with me. In *mine*, I beheld the possible as opposed to the actual and gave Him my will to lead in that way. That *was* the best I could do. But it has proven not only to be enough but to be enough for triumph!

Now Paul didn't say conversely that our strength becomes weakness. Of course not. But it must go through the same process to be productive. Our talents are worthless as offerings to God if not properly evaluated and presented to Him for His special touch. He accepts the availability of them and turns us loose to reap the harvest of them for *Him!*

*Ah! And then there follows perhaps the most exciting adventure of all: As God and I get acquainted with ME, He gives me, more and more, the fantastic privilege of choice.* The personality moves out of the realm of legislation into freedom! I get to help Him, if you will, determine what shall mold my life!

Abraham Lincoln once said, "Those people are happy who choose to be."

As surely as an artist chooses colors and brushes, the picture I have of myself, and the one I paint for those around me to see, is painted by the choices I make day by day by day. Elementary. However, the more I allow God to reveal me to me, the wiser my choices are, the fewer mistakes I make, the more productive my strengths are, and my painting reflects deeper colors, greater dimension, and more perfect shading. Praise the Lord for that!

It was my joy to have heard Dr. Hardy C. Powers preach

many times. None of his sermons have meant more to me over the years than one he preached using a very simple illustration as his format. He told of a personal experience while in Sydney, Australia, on business for his church.

He had left his hotel room for a short walk. While attempting to cross the narrow street, he stepped from the curb a little too soon; a very small truck turned the corner a little too sharply, and the thumb of his right hand suffered the consequence. It hurt! He was embarrassed. He took his thumb back to his room to nurse it. And while doing so, he decided it was no big deal. In fact, he concluded he probably would never ever tell it. He also came to the conclusion that if he was going to allow himself to be hit by a truck it was going to have to be a big one before he would own up to it!

Applying his thoughts in his sermon, he yearned that those of us listening would be careful to *choose* what we permit to derail us. He pointed out the uselessness of throwing in the towel because of minor obstacles and petty differences. God is, he preached, capable of giving us a knowledge and understanding of what we can cope with internally. God and I . . . knowing . . . revealing . . . choosing!

One of the nicest presents we ever received as a family was a gift certificate for Christmas dinner at the classiest, most prestigious restaurant in our large city. We made reservations. Not having been there before, we were unaware that the men were required to wear jackets and ties. Our experience with this sort of thing was very limited! My husband and son were wearing jackets but not ties. I guess because it was Christmas, the maitre d' finally decided to let us dine. I was exercised! Not at the establishment, but at our lack of knowledge.

"Why didn't you wear ties?" I asked, trying to make someone responsible. My whole Christmas day was being ruined.

My teenage son looked at me calmly and said, "Mother, cool it!"

"Don't you *ever* get upset?" I asked.

"Yes," he replied, "but not about such silly, stupid things as whether or not I have on a tie!"

A long, hard look at myself! That prompted me to begin a list that I call Pat's beatitudes. Here are some of them.

I shall *choose* not to be destroyed by the petty things of life. That is why it is valuable to know what gets *to* me. I can learn to avoid those situations as much as possible or discipline myself to handle the ones I can do nothing about.

I shall *choose* not to be ensnared by the negatives. I once heard Mrs. Earl Mosteller relate a beautiful illustration of this point. A native girl on their field of missionary assignment had made a wall plaque for the Mostellers from two gorgeous butterflies. For realism the young girl had included a small branch and a little bug. Shortly after it had been hung on the missionary's wall, another native girl walked into the room, looked at the plaque and exclaimed, "Oooo, look at the *bug!*"

Lord, make me respond to the beauty, to the best, to positives! Help me be oblivious to the bugs! At least, give me the insight to keep them in their place.

I shall *choose* not to be mentally petrified by my weaknesses, either in the sense of being scared, or of being "dead." I shall not flee from them as running from a snake, nor shall I embrace them as I would a soft puppy. I shall get them into focus.

I shall *choose* not to be overindulged by, or afraid of, my strengths. Thank You, Lord, for them. Help me to see the obvious ones and to discover the hidden. I shall handle them all carefully, keeping in mind that they are a reflection of Your goodness.

Recently, I enrolled with a friend in a very interesting self-improvement course, primarily because I knew the instructor well. It is what I term a Christian charm course. It was fun, informative, and helpful. During one class our instructor quoted a famous Hollywood makeup expert as saying, "There are no such things as ugly women, only lazy ones."

My version reads: There are no spiritually poverty-stricken, inferior, worthless Christians because of God, only those who choose to be. God believes in me. He said so! I choose to believe in me!

So I take everything there is of me: potential, weakness, strength, choice, and willingness, and tie them with a ribbon. But wait, the package is not complete. My best is me *and* God's resources!

Some years ago a wonderful film was made based on a true story. It was called *The Touch of the Master's Hand.* Briefly, it was the story of a man who had died leaving no survivors but a huge estate made up mostly of art treasures. The will provided for an auction to dispose of the collection. People from all over Europe gathered to bid. But no one seemed to want the first offering, which was a crude painting done by the deceased himself of his son who had preceded him in death.

After a long, awkward silence the piece was purchased by a longtime household servant who had known the son.

"And now the auction is concluded," declared the auctioneer.

Stunned silence.

"Because, you see, the will says that whoever cares enough to buy the painting of the son may have the entire estate!"

Colossians (2:9-10) says, "You have everything when you have Christ!" (TLB). I do not believe I do it disservice to add that when you care enough to give of your best, you have all of God's resources, too! They are: the will of the Father, the experience of the Son, and the work of the Holy Spirit.

After all has been said and done about God's will for our

lives, there is one glaring conclusion: He desires our best good! And His resources are unlimited in bringing that to pass. They are more available and pure than the very air we breathe!

But wait! His desire is coupled with Christ's experience! He *has been there!* Where? Wherever it is that we are! Our best is not complete without appropriating the vast knowledge Christ has of the human experience! He knows where we are, and He knows what we are feeling.

And as if that isn't enough, the Holy Spirit is ours to empower us to be victorious no matter what paths we may be directed to walk. He sustains us while we make good and better into best.

Such a package deal!

Before I close this chapter, I must tell you I can still hear my father say, "Don't settle for less than your best."

"OK, Daddy, I get the message. But you are in heaven now, and with your glorified mind you surely know that there are times when it isn't easy. I *am* trying. But sometimes the lack of energy, an overwhelming responsibility not easily accepted, the devil's subtle whispering that I am incapable, ineffective, and just plain stupid, shortcircuits the project. But hear this! I promise I will not allow myself to *settle* for less! And God has promised He won't *let* me!"

# 4

# For Then He Will Have the Personal Satisfaction of Work Well Done

IT HAS NEVER BEEN EASY for me to receive gifts, especially what I consider expensive ones. On one occasion I objected sincerely to a very generous gift because, for one thing, I was afraid my thank you would not seem to equal the size of the gift. The giver said to me, "Pat, we must all learn to give, but we must learn how to receive as well."

That is exactly the way most of us handle compliments. We are good at giving them. Or we should be. But few of us are really comfortable in receiving them.

Certainly the following is not standard behavior, but I would like to tell you about the philosophy of one of our friends. In the early years of our acquaintance he would respond to "You look very nice today," with "I know it!" He would never use the usual, "Thank you."

One day we decided to bring up the subject.

"Look," he said, "I spend lots of time in the morning getting dressed, putting on just the rightly coordinated clothes, doing the best I can with my hair and mustache, shaving just right. Now why should I say thank you for something I am quite capable of doing, have made a deliberate effort to accomplish, and ought to do in the first place?"

We still shake our heads a little wondering how a sincere Christian who has had a lucrative career and raised a fine family could do so with such a streak of seeming arrogance!

But let's turn the coin over. Since God has indicated that there is such a thing as a work well done, how do we explain our reactions when someone else thinks we have done well and says so?

"Oh, it was nothing."

"Someone else could have done it better."

"I really didn't do much."

"I really am not very capable, it just happened."

We are treading on a very fine line! I know that. God would not have us be haughty, proud of self, or braggadocios. A spirit of superiority would never be condoned by Him.

Remember this old fable?

A frog sat on a cold lily pad eavesdropping on the conversation of two birds.

"I'm cold," said one.

"Me too," said the other. "Let's fly South where it is warm."

"I want to go," cried the frog. "*I'm* cold!"

"Silly frog," said the first bird, "you can't fly."

The frog frowned. Suddenly, he jumped to shore.

"Look! Here is a piece of string! If each of you will fly holding an end of the string in your beak, I can grab hold of the middle with my mouth and you can fly me to the warm South!"

They worked together until the idea became reality. Up, up, and away!

Looking up from their plowing, two farmers saw the ingenious scheme in operation.

Said one, "Now, who ever thought up a thing like that?"

"*I did!*" said the frog! And of course, his boastful pride cost him his life.

God will and does provide the tools for ingenious work

and witness on our part. The secret of spiritual growth by way of accomplishment is to be quick in giving credit where credit is due: *To Him.* The stream cannot deny the fountain. Therein lies the determination of what is and is not pride. The creature credits the Creator for everything! And it is possible to do that to others without involving our abilities *or* the lack of them. For instance:

"Hasn't He given wonderful insights?"

"I couldn't have done it without His help!"

"Isn't it amazing what God does when we let Him?"

God is not a contradiction. He either means what He says, or He isn't God. And He has promised all the ingredients for a job well done. What are they?

> He has promised sufficiency.
> He has promised strength.
> He has promised guidance.
> He has promised understanding.

Best of all, he has promised a harvest of even the smallest effort: a mite, a cup of water, a song in the night!

It isn't stretching a point in the least to say that a work well done begins by believing God's Word. His Word is so full of promises and examples that no work need be ungrounded or unsupported by Him!

The Word of God, of course, can be incorporated into any book on any subject. But it is so applicable here. For the more I read and *accept* His Word, the more intimately I know Him and the less amazed I am at what He does or what He asks me to do. And His will for me certainly becomes clearer! Reading His Word and obeying His will are prerequisites to doing a job well and reaping the personal satisfaction promised. For a job well done by me is not judged as such by how well I articulated the message, or made the poster, or sang the song, but rather, that I *claimed* His resources, *gave* Him mine, and *applied* my energies to that "best" goal!

God does have guarantees! They are not specific results,

explosions in the sky, adulation, or even recognition, but, as stated in this promise, personal satisfaction. That, if we can only grasp it, is far-and-away better than "all of the above."

Paul began this particular scripture by admonishing the hearer to "be doing." It is only while we are "doing" that this promise of personal satisfaction is valid. Surely we know that does not mean physical activity alone. The prayer life is "doing." Mental growth and stimulation is "doing." Behind-the-scenes organizing is "doing." But His promises are always predicated on some deliberate action on our part.

One must believe that if recognizing that we have done a work well is difficult, accepting that God approves our feeling personal satisfaction must be next to impossible! It *must* be carnal to feel good about ourselves, to encounter a deep-down glow of satisfaction in the work God has helped us do.

I was enjoying listening to a certain lecturer because she had the natural ability to make her point through her wonderful gift of humor.

"I sat at lunch with my friend," she was saying, "and finally got the nerve to ask her weight. When she told me 112, I looked aghast and informed her that 112 was *not* a weight, it was a blood pressure!"

I identified so thoroughly that I laughed louder than I should have.

The class was on weight control. I was now a lifetime member. Besides meaning that I had, through much self-denial, reached my goal weight, I was thinking it must also mean that one spends a lifetime putting it on and taking it off!

On this particular day the leader suggested that each of us conduct a mental survey to determine why we were there. Why *was* I here? There was no doubt that the results looked better. I was sure my friends and family were proud of me, and being able to buy something from the smaller sizes on the rack was almost as much fun as eating a doughnut! But I knew that those kinds of motivation would not have gotten me this far.

I turned my thoughts back to the time I had begun. True, I had gotten started because I thought I would look better. Isn't that what all the magazines say? Beauty is in the eye of the beholder, and every eye these days sees beauty in thinness. But I remembered the day during my dieting when that didn't matter. Who cared I was tired of the whole routine!

Thumbing listlessly through some related material one day, I ran across an article dealing with the psychological aspects of weight reduction. The bottom line was that success in losing weight comes because one does it for *oneself!* Not because someone else drives you to it, or badgers you about it, or makes fun of your appearance. Those may be contributing factors, but they will not in themselves carry you over the long haul. It is done primarily for one's own sake! There it was. The impetus I needed to keep at it. I was going to do this for me. Not selfishly, or as a martyr, but for the personal satisfaction and resultant sense of accomplishment that would come because of my discipline.

Perhaps that illustration gives us some insight as to why people "burn out," even in secular work. Lots of good reasons can get us started initially, but, especially in God's work, we bog down along the way because other reasons and other people overshadow the most important and lasting motivation: this is my challenge, given to me by God, given *back* to Him by me for His assistance and affirmation!

In losing weight, personal satisfaction translates into feeling good about myself; a job well done for the Christian expands that to feeling good about *God* and myself. There is spiritual growth . . . new energy . . . new appreciation for me as God's created. The work given to me by Him is not *for* me; it must be for the advancement and glorification of Him and His kingdom, but the reward of personal satisfaction should be no less intense! Rather, it should be greater than any human recompense!

Having had the honor of speaking to groups of ministers' wives several times, I've also had the honor of listening to them, hearing their thoughts, sharing the verbalization of their distresses. One of the things I feel strongly about as a result is this: if I had the power to grant one wish for all ministers' wives everywhere it would be that they could do what they do in God's vineyard strictly from one motivation—a strong conviction that that is what *God* would have them do. Not because it is expected, or because they are forced to, but because through their prayer life they have found their "niche" with God.

A light bulb just turned on. Since writing the above and rereading it, I see no reason for that wish to be limited to the minister's wife! Oh, that "all God's chillun" could enjoy that privilege! "Here I am, Lord. What do You have available for someone with my ability?"

It isn't that personal satisfaction cannot come by doing the expected or the mandatory, but that the greatest level of self-approval comes when I can affirm within myself that this is what He had in mind for me . . . for the moment . . . for a lifetime. Knowing one has carried out God's directive lays a foundation and gives a perspective that nothing else can. Note: I would not wish that our activities necessarily be in areas that we *want* them to be in. Doing something *just* because we want to is stagnation. So is volunteering for something that we know very well we can excel at, if that is the *only* time we offer our services. God is multifaceted! He is not limited to giving personal satisfaction only when talents are involved.

That brings to mind another myth. Why must we feel that God only and always leads us into service predominantly distasteful to us? Must righteousness always be coupled with hardship and tasks that I really dislike?

"I love this aspect of His work, therefore it can't be what He would have me do!"

I'm convinced that God wants to give us the desires of our hearts in the assignments He gives. More than we ever dream! Sometimes He doesn't care at all if we get into the cookie jar! (Although He probably won't allow us to *live* there.)

One of our friends knew a gentleman who lamented the fact that he could do nothing but make money! I think I could handle that problem, don't you? He *loved* making money. But surely, he reasoned, he had missed God's will because he had never been able to teach, preach, or reach. Our wise friend assured him that God's kingdom needed money. Because his business had long ago been dedicated to God and he had been very generous with his assets, and since God had given him the assurance of a job well done, he should go on making money for the Lord. The personal satisfaction will remain as long as his priority system keeps the Lord as president of the corporation!

Then there is the young man, so typical of a similar inherited misconception, who came to my husband and asked for counsel concerning his relationship to the Lord.

"Something *has* to be wrong with me spiritually," he reasoned, "because my business is doing so well."

We smile at that, but do you know anyone who has looked with suspicion on someone else who has been financially successful, judging that they could not possibly be totally honest with God and man?

A work well done is not limited to certain areas of endeavor. That is, unless it is specifically forbidden in God's Word. A work well done is assured when we (1) understand the directions, (2) refuse to alter the instructions, and (3) apply to it the very best God has given us.

My children shouldn't be told this, but I did participate in extra extracurricular activities in college. How many times

I got caught is none of their business! On one occasion several of us in our dormitory were called upon to sit in the dean of women's living room for the purpose of justifying our latest escapade. Such a sober lady! She never did see the humor and levied punishment much too severe for the nature of the crime. After a lengthy reprimand and even longer instructions, she went around the room several times, calling each of us by name, asking, "Do *you* understand!" Even today when any of us who were present get together, someone invariably asks, "Do *you* understand?" with heavy emphasis on the YOUUU!

The Creator has given mankind the instructions. They are individualized to *each* person through personal relationship one on one, Creator and created. I can almost hear Him saying, "Do *you* understand?"

I just can't decide which translation of Prov. 4:13 I prefer, so why don't I share my two favorites with you?

> Hold on to instruction, do not let it go; guard it well, for it is your life *(NIV)*.

> Carry out my instructions; don't forget them, for they will lead you to real living *(TLB)*.

He does not make me accountable for the comprehension of another. He loves me enough to be sure that what He says makes sense to *me*, and He is patient until understanding is my very own.

Periodically, we make it necessary for that patience to extend past understanding, past arguing (as Moses did), and past all our suggested alterations of the instructions. Moses should have known he wasn't any match for the Lord, but then, he wasn't as smart as modern man!

Understanding, obedience, and action! Personal satisfaction follows as surely and as naturally as pounds follow calories!

Ever read a book when you felt that the last paragraph of a chapter was just a winding down of that particular thought? Well, this one does not have a postscript. The best is included here at the last. This is the most important. For besides the obvious results of work well done . . .

> the young mother who has found new perspective because you kept her child and freed her to her thoughts;
> the elderly person who smiles again because you took time to give attention;
> the gratifying response to the well-organized, fruitful banquet you planned;
> the children in your Sunday School class who believe in a heavenly being because you have told them He exists and now look upon you as their link to Him;
> the few, or hundreds, who bow at an altar because God gave you a masterful sermon, a profound speech, or simple testimony

. . . the greatest outcome of all comes after we have done our best, have realized a job well done, and have experienced the personal satisfaction that God gives. For the spirit of man will respond with "Let's do it again, Lord! You and I are a team. Lord, You coach and I will bat!"

During the game I will need to catch my breath. He knows that! But if I am willing He assures the home runs and base hits. And even when I strike out, it will be with the personal satisfaction that *He* sent me into the game!!

# 5

# And Won't Need to Compare Himself with Someone Else

My MOTHER was not thin. Never by any stretch of the polyester! And I would be rich today if I had a dollar (inflation, you know) for every time she said to me, "Am I as fat as that lady over there?" Most of the time I didn't answer for fear of endangering myself. For, before ever turning to look at the woman in question, I knew she was carrying lots of pounds. Mother would never have compared herself to anyone thin. Mother's generation thought anyone two inches wide was unhealthy and apt to reach the pearly gates long before her heavy-set, even-aged counterpart. To put her own size on the line with someone thinner would not have soothed her conscience. And that is a great deal of what comparison is all about: soothing the conscience, stroking the ego, and reassuring decisions and actions.

Not too long ago our family was discussing the attributes of one of the current television stars whose obvious assets had been printed almost to the nth degree and whose posters had papered walls of mansions, dormitories, and huts. I was sincere (I think!) when I remarked, "I don't think she is pretty at all." My son smiled a tolerant grin and replied, "Mom, that's sour grapes." Perhaps! And that's another part of the makeup of comparison—sour grapes!

Funny what we remember over long periods of time. It

has been years since I have seen a particular television program, yet one scene from it comes back to me often.

The star of the weekly situation comedy found herself attending an elite social function resplendent with very important people. Her escort, also her admission ticket, was a photographer assigned to catch on film the bejewelled and beglittered. Going off to do his job, he left her with instructions just to "mingle." And mingle she did. All around the great ballroom she wandered in and out of the crowd, audibly mumbling, "Mingle, mingle, mingle, mingle." No one paid any attention. Some nodded, "Uh huh" and there was an occasional, "Oh, really?" thrown in her direction, but no one ever *really* saw or heard her.

I see in that scene a parallel to much of today's impersonal society. Scores of us go through life, in and out of the crowds, measuring, measuring, measuring. Comparison contributes much to many of the horrible, far-reaching sociological ills of our day. Peer pressure. Divorce. Financial disaster. And the frightening epidemic of teenage suicide stems, in part, from the demand on them to measure, measure, measure. No one listens or sees. And so the alternative is to end it all. A "simple" way to get out of the race.

Whoa! I didn't intend to plunge headlong into the negative aspects of the subject. So let me hasten to say that comparison. in and of itself, is not negative. It is not wrong. Not totally unfruitful. In fact, without it I cannot recognize growth. Neither can you. But Paul's admonition does not condemn comparison. It is the *need* to compare that we should free ourselves from.

Suppose we discuss some of the reasons we feel a need to compare ourselves in the first place.

Comparison is unhealthy for us when we use it as a tool to excuse our own slothfulness.

"If I had so and so's time and money, I could do such and such . . ."

"There is no use for me to try to do that, I can't do as good a job as . . ."

"The whole thing is out of my league . . ."

We become trapped in the net of "do little or nothing" because our energy has been robbed from us, *by* us, because we have made a comparison and found ourselves wanting in our own eyes. Of course, the mistake is that we have used someone else's assets as our measuring stick.

Hand in hand with that pitfall is the one in which we try to justify our present state of affairs by a comparison to someone or something we perceive as being in a worse condition. Sometimes our perception is actually correct. But the harm comes when we stroke our egos with the inferiority, misfortune, or handicaps of others.

Isn't it an unforgettable experience when God speaks to us about something in such a clear way that there is absolutely no mistaking His voice? Great! Great, that is, if we don't turn our backs! I had run to my room one day to tell Him all about the treatment I had received from a lady who had been very unfair to me. He told me He already knew about it!

"Lord, I know I handled this in a very stupid way, but *she* was *so* wrong. If *she* hadn't misunderstood so terribly, *she* wouldn't have created this situation. *She* has a problem, Lord. Please help *her!*"

No mistake . . . it was the Lord's voice: "You're right, but let's not concern ourselves with her. Let's talk about *you.*"

God would not let me get by with unbecoming behavior just because it was not as extreme as someone else's. How easy and convenient to remind God that someone else needs help because it makes our own shortcomings seem less significant in comparison.

Perhaps there is no comparison more damaging than the comparison that seeks to change the rock-bottom, basic structure of personal nature. Read that again—the devil is trying to keep it a secret!

"I *must* be like . . ."

My recollections of the church of my childhood are centered around a wonderful body of believers who loved the Lord and shouted it, literally, to the world. Everyone was emotional. Everyone prayed loudly. The off-key sounds of the boisterous singing was not that of untrained voices, but the music of those whose singing had given way to shouting! They laughed. They walked, sometimes ran, the aisles praising the Lord with raised hands, bulletins, hankies, and babies. I loved it! Still do!

But shortly after settling my own business with the Lord, Satan and I began a long, continuing argument about my emotional response (or lack of it I should say) to religion.

"If you really knew the Lord," he would whisper, "*you* would shout, or at *least* utter an amen now and then."

"I wish I could," I assured him and me.

"Well, just you mark it down, you could if you *really* had something!"

I even agreed one day.

Then God cast His vote! The weapon I needed for rebuttal was right under my nose! It was my grandmother! I can see Grandma laughing at being called a "weapon"! She was so tiny she would be hard-pressed to threaten anyone.

Grandma was very much a saint. Saintliest of the saintly. No one disputed that. Grandma was also very English. Very reserved. No one disputed that, either. And when God voted to affirm that I, indeed, had a personal relationship with Him, He wrote a P.S. on the ballot reminding me and my adversary that Grandma was as quiet as a mouse in church!

What a lost cause, trying to make myself be what someone else is!

I tried that once! Mention the words *sophistication, elegance,* and *poise* and flashing across my mind will be a picture of one lady who, for me, has been the epitome of that description for a long time. I first knew her as a minister's wife, then as a woman, a wife, a mother, and a grandmother. The picture never has changed.

I said to her daughter once, "Someday I want to be like your mother!"

Her daughter, whom I love very much and who knows *me* very well replied, "Forget it. You'll never make it." And I haven't. But something I have made is the marvelous discovery that great qualities in others are terrific to assess, admire, and learn from. I can even risk comparing myself—standing alongside to be measured—just so long as I guard carefully against the temptation to spend my energies making myself into an unnatural likeness of that one so admired.

One more step in this direction. The ultimate tragedy stands before us in the person who has allowed comparison to become a way of life—preoccupation.

Among our friends is a family we have always enjoyed being with when our paths have managed to cross. Over the years we have compared notes regarding the development of our children. Two of theirs have provided them with great contrasting emotions. One has brought great joy, another great sorrow. In a nutshell, one of the girls has suffered both actual and imagined misery because she has found no way to lead her life on her own ground. She cannot seem to function without comparing herself and all that happens to her with that of her sister's life. And the great waste is that she has such latent abilities of her own, capable of surpassing some of her sister's. Oh, that she could be delivered from a life of comparing air and steel!

One last observation. It comes with a prayer that you will still like me! Comparison is a terrific "asset" for putting people down under the guise of enlightening our audience. The performance being praised to me may not even directly involve me. The person being described in glowing terms may not even be an acquaintance. By innuendo I can reaffirm my own opinions and in so doing make myself an easier person (supposedly) for me to live with. How easy to belittle someone else's talent, to remind the listener of the flaw in that other one's perfection, or to point out the discrepancies in another's doctrinal position because it gives ample opportunity to measure ourselves and remain secure. God forgive us! Again and again!

Let's get down to the brass tacks! The nail may not be brass, but let's hit it on the head anyway. Comparison is alive and well because we do not accept ourselves. We spend countless, anxious moments comparing ourselves because we do not accept ourselves where we are.

I do not believe self-acceptance is ever 100 percent accomplished. If that were possible, wouldn't we be stunted in our spiritual growth? Genuine self-knowledge and acceptance incorporates an unending reach for additional development. God in His *mercy* will not allow us to graduate; to do so is impossible, anyway, because the course of study is inexhaustible!

One of the most important statements in this book for me, personally, is found in the introduction. My object has never been to write a how-to book, although that would guarantee the possibility of a sequel since a how-to manual can never be conclusive or definitive. Progress is continually excavating the territory and mining new nuggets of instruction. And who of us dares establish a status quo posture on any level just because we think we have covered the subject?

So, the following are "let's do" proposals. They are memos tacked to my heart's door. When I have mastered them, I will let you know, but don't expect to hear from me soon, if ever! I cannot be sure that they will transform your life. I hope they make a difference. I *can* say that they have had a significant bearing on mine.

For starters, eliminate from your thinking the "if" syndrome:

"If I were married . . ."

"If I were single . . ."

"If I were rich . . ."

"If I were pretty . . ."

"If I were talented . . ."

"If I had friends . . ."

"If I didn't have children . . ."

"If I were a strong Christian . . ."

"If my husband were a Christian . . ."

"If I hadn't been so mistreated . . ."

To complete this list would produce a volume rivaling an unabridged Webster's! To be able to record the effects all of us would experience by refusing to let this small word short-circuit our lives would produce an even larger work. *If* I were profound I could make you see its force! Come on, smile at the application!

Learn from experience, but adamantly refuse to be dominated by regret. Hindsight *is* better in most cases, but to *embrace* regret is to impair today's vision and frighten us away from foresight. In the self-acceptance cabinet, regret is filed under "Learning Experiences: Now God's Responsibility."

That folder is just next to "Cooperate with the Inevitable!" Acceptance is most difficult when that which we cannot change is involved. That is, when the changing does not lie within my power. Chafing about it is akin to the burr in the saddle. It only serves to irritate. Banging one's head against a brick wall smacks of childishness; it will only produce a headache, it will not affect the brick! (I am smiling a little to myself right now, thinking of a few I have known who might be hardheaded enough to do so!)

Go on a safari to find something entirely yours! That may be difficult since a huge percentage of all that we do or have is intertwined with others and their welfare. Invest in *your* stock! I have at times. And I have "dividends" around my house from various adventures: essays written for "just-for-fun" college classes, ceramic pieces and craft productions (some evident, some hidden), even a bowling trophy that brings a loud laugh because getting it was such a fluke! They aren't valuable, really, except that they represent investments in my sanity and nervous system.

Do yourself a favor: make a list of people who intimidate you and follow it with a diligent effort to discover why. People who intimidate us are always those we see as being more ——— than we are. You fill in the blank, and in so doing you have taken step one in ridding yourself of their effect on you.

Overcoming intimidation is not brought about by our desire to change the other person or to make ourselves like them. I have made great strides when I accept what and who I am in my own right. Margery Wilson again: "Our ability to be un-self-conscious and genuinely interested in other people is wholly dependent on our estimate of ourselves!"[1] Self-acceptance in the Lord cannot be surpassed! It will not intimidate, nor will it be threatened. It will bless and be blessed because God is no respecter of persons.

O Lord, deliver me from the urge to impress others! What fun I have remembering times I've made a mess trying to impress someone or to be sophisticated. Oh, I've made an impression! Somewhere, someplace, someone is thinking of me in terms of stupidity and/or klutziness! Might as well laugh at myself!

There is a captivating beauty in sophistication when it is real. Some of my friends are stimulating examples. But for both those who are and those who are not, trying to impress is a dead giveaway, because now there is no hiding the fact that one is not comfortable with herself.

We may succumb to false pretense, *the deadliest enemy of our self-esteem*, because we fear "the real me" may not be

---

1. Wilson, *Woman You Want to Be*, 151.

good enough to meet the situation at hand. The attempt to make an impression other than what we are belies our own insecurity and places us squarely on thin ice. Others may not even know. But we will and shall be restless about it. Really, now, why "dress up" our personalities if our "wardrobe" only includes casual? If we do that just to impress, we had better be careful: we may fall off our high heels!

Look at the other side of the street. The message is the same! Sophistication sometimes cannot bring itself to certain degrees of casualness and should not self-inflict the pain of trying to do so. Sincerity and genuineness wear all kinds of clothes!

Learn to give what *you* need. I would love to flourish that on a marquee and emphasize it with twinkling lights and moving spotlights!

If you need friends, ask God to help you be a friend. If you are lonely, find a lonely person to share some time with. If you are hurting financially, spend a little something on someone else. If you are discouraged, seek out someone to encourage. This may seem impossible, but if you are ill, write or dictate a note to another who is suffering physically. If you need to grow spiritually, share a meaningful scripture and/or an answer to prayer (no matter how insignificant it may seem) with one who is a new Christian or one struggling to keep the faith!

If you are divorced and reason confirms there is no possible reconciliation, put it behind you as much as possible. Deal with the residue of legal matters and family connections fairly, but build anew emotionally. Ask God to discipline your thinking until your point of reference for living is from *this* day, not from what once was. It is impossible to build a strong, lovely structure on a crumbled base!

If you are widowed, the same exercise holds help. Cherish the memories while resisting the beckoning call of the past to be comfortable only with it. To accept your present state and to make plans for today and tomorrow is not betrayal of any kind. It is not disloyalty or selfishness. It is survival!

Finally, make a list of what you would like to be personally. Mental enumeration at this point is not enough. Write it down! Consult with the Lord. Beginning with His Word, supplement His store of graces with Christian material that will help you find and develop that peculiar, unique person God created at your conception. It is never too late. Today is *always* a good day to grow!

Paul said we won't need to compare ourselves with someone else. Ever have someone reply to your inquiry of "How are you?" with "As compared to what?" I have. It brings me up with a start! But I like it because it makes me think. Well, let's see now . . . as compared to what? My neighbor . . . my sister . . . my husband's great-aunt's best friend . . . my alcoholic acquaintance . . . my socialite friend . . . Miss America . . . Princess Diana? The only answer of substance will be, "As compared to me, myself, and I, and what I am and CAN be in the Lord."

Comparison is a great yardstick. If used properly, it will allow me to stretch way beyond its "three feet" length; for in measuring me with me I shall just keep on growin' and growin'.

Mirror, mirror, on the wall . . .
       sure enough,
         I'm six feet tall!

# 6

# A Mirror
# by Any Other Name . . .

I HOLD in my hand a mirror. I see in it an individual so special that the Almighty God himself declared that the wealth of the world could not compare in value! I cannot fathom that. *Me, valuable?*

Ah, I recall an equally staggering statement from His Word: I was not only made by Him, but *for* Him. And just today I read in Ephesians that "because of what Christ has done we have become gifts to God that he delights in" (1:11, TLB). I look again. *Me? A gift?*

Incredibly, His Word goes on to say that since He loved us so much we can become His children and "God can always point to us as examples of how very, very rich his kindness is, as shown in all he has done for us through Christ Jesus" (2:7, TLB). Another look. *Me? An example?* Mmmmm . . .

Will Rogers, the down-home, tongue-in-cheek philosopher, decided, "God must have loved the ordinary people, He made so many of us." An easy-to-listen-to contemporary gospel song prods us to remember that "God uses ordinary people."

But wait a minute! Others, perhaps feeling a little protective of God's omnipotence, object, insisting that God has never made *anything* ordinary.

Who to believe? Probably both. Ordinary is determined in large measure by quantity. Diamonds, gold, sable, and great statesmen alike are not thought of as ordinary because of their rarity. In that sense, God did make us ordinary. There sure are a lot of us! What God can and does do in us, however, is never ordinary. He will make us special, one-of-a-kind replicas of His multifaceted image and nature.

Surely He used ordinary things. He used clay pots once in lieu of those fashionable Grecian urns that couldn't have been very far away. The prancing steed was bypassed in favor of a donkey on one occasion. He even spat into some dirt one day to make a healing salve. Surely He knew about plastic surgery and antibiotics! Maybe yachts weren't "in," but I wish He could have found something besides those dirty fishing boats!

God had already acquired the habit of using ordinary people as far back as Genesis. One of the most ordinary was Abraham. (I can hear the uproar!) It certainly does not require great skill to do what God called Abraham to do. His initial approach to him was, "I want you to *walk* with me."

Moses was just such a man, too. For starters, he was a fugitive, had a speech impediment, and was scared to death of both his own people and those with whom he had been raised. And if *he* was ordinary, his rod was even more so! There were only *thousands* of them in Midian!

Yes, God sure has used lots of ordinary things and people. With one little difference though: He never did ask to use *things*. He just said things like "Bring Me the pots" and "If anyone questions you concerning the donkey, tell them the master has need of it." But He never has used a *person* without asking and getting permission to do so. He will never change us from ordinary to a rare likeness of Him without our consent!

But, oh, the transformation when we say yes!

Each instant, hour, day, and year becomes a vessel in

which the perfecting process leads me along a path that encounters happiness, exhilaration, sorrow, tragedy, pain, vision, and all *kinds* of experiences, with numerous wayside stops for self-evaluation.

That's called life!

Paul was excited with the anticipation of the end result. "We confidently and joyfully look forward to actually becoming all that God has had in mind for us to be" (Rom. 5:2, TLB).

J. C. Brumfield, in a tiny, wonderful booklet titled *Comfort for Troubled Christians* shed this light on what we call life. An old refiner was asked by a visitor, "How does the refiner know when the fire has done its perfect work?" He answered, "See how I sit by the fire?" The stranger answered, "Yes." Then he said, "See how I bend over the pot?" Again the stranger said, "Yes, but how do you know when there has been just the right amount of heat?" The old refiner looked up and said, "When I see my own reflection."[1]

The man or woman in whom God sees His own reflection ceases to be ordinary. Wherever they are found, in the kitchen, at the office, in the schoolroom, at the podium, on the farm, or at the helm, they are *now* rare!

Dr. George Duncan writes:

> Most Christians are more concerned about the redeeming task than the revealing task. Do you know the story of the small girl whose mother found her drawing one day, and asked her what she was drawing? She got the surprising answer "I'm drawing God." "Oh, you can't do that," said her mother; "You don't know what God is like; nobody knows what God is like!" She got an even more startling reply: "Well, Mummy, they will know when I'm finished!" Will they know when you have finished, and when I have finished? I wonder. If we have been sent to reveal as well as to redeem, what image do

---

1. J. C. Brumfield, *Comfort for Troubled Christians* (Chicago: Moody Press. Moody Bible Institute, n.d.) Used by permission.

we project in the minds of men? Is it the image of the God who loved and still loves the world?[2]

An old fable begins with "once upon a time."

In a little village lived a little man in a little house. Everyone in the little village knew where the little house was that housed the little man, for he was known to be *very* wise. None had fooled or stumped him yet.

One day, three little boys sat beneath a tree, combining their imaginations to determine a way to pose a problem to the little man that he could not answer.

"I know," said one. "We will catch a small bird. I will carry it to his house in my hand. I shall ask him if the bird is alive. If he says it is, I will crush out its life in my fist. If he says it isn't, I shall set it free. Either way, he will be wrong!"

"Perfect," was the agreement.

And so they did as they had planned.

The little man hobbled out his door in response to their knocking. The young boy stood, fortified by his friends, clenching the bird in his closed hand.

"Tell me," said he, "is this bird in my hand dead or alive?"

The little man stroked his beard as if finding his wisdom there.

"The answer, my son, lies with you. It is *your* hand!"

The mirror is in your hand. What do you see? Reflections of hurts, mistakes, insecurity, victories, blame, revenge, joy, peace, weakness, ability, failure, good work, love, help . . . God?

What will you do with them?

The answer
    my new friend
       lies with you.
          It is *your* hand!

---

2. George Duncan, *It Could Be Your Problem* (London and Glasgow: Pickering and Inglis, 1977), 6.